OECD ECONOMIC SURVEYS

2002-2003

Ireland

OECD

ORGANISATION FOR ECONOMIC CO-OPERATION AND DEVELOPMENT

ORGANISATION FOR ECONOMIC CO-OPERATION AND DEVELOPMENT

Pursuant to Article 1 of the Convention signed in Paris on 14th December 1960, and which came into force on 30th September 1961, the Organisation for Economic Co-operation and Development (OECD) shall promote policies designed:

- to achieve the highest sustainable economic growth and employment and a rising standard of living in member countries, while maintaining financial stability, and thus to contribute to the development of the world economy;
- to contribute to sound economic expansion in member as well as non-member countries in the process of economic development; and
- to contribute to the expansion of world trade on a multilateral, non-discriminatory basis in accordance with international obligations.

The original member countries of the OECD are Austria, Belgium, Canada, Denmark, France, Germany, Greece, Iceland, Ireland, Italy, Luxembourg, the Netherlands, Norway, Portugal, Spain, Sweden, Switzerland, Turkey, the United Kingdom and the United States. The following countries became members subsequently through accession at the dates indicated hereafter: Japan (28th April 1964), Finland (28th January 1969), Australia (7th June 1971), New Zealand (29th May 1973), Mexico (18th May 1994), the Czech Republic (21st December 1995), Hungary (7th May 1996), Poland (22nd November 1996), Korea (12th December 1996) and the Slovak Republic (14th December 2000). The Commission of the European Communities takes part in the work of the OECD (Article 13 of the OECD Convention).

Publié également en français.

Table of Contents

•••••

Boxes

Tables

Annex

Figures

BASIC STATISTICS OF IRELAND

THE LAND

Area (thousand sq.km)	70	Population of major cities, 1996[1] census (thousands):	
Agricultural area, 1995, as per cent of total area	57	Dublin (Country and Co. Borough)	1 057
		Cork (Co. Borough)	127
		Limerick (Co. Borough)	52

THE PEOPLE

Population in thousands (April 2002)[1]	3 897	Net emigration: average 1993-95	2 333
Number of inhabitants per sq.km	56	Net immigration: average 1996-99	16 075
		Net immigration: average 2000-2002	25 033
Increase in population: annual average 1996-2002	291 249	Total labour force, Sept.-Nov. 2002 (thousands)	1 855
Natural increase in population: annual average 2001-2002	27 550	Civilian employment, Sept.-Nov. 2002 (thousands):	
		Agriculture, forestry and fishing	120
		Industry and construction	493
		Other sectors	1 158

THE GOVERNMENT

Public current expenditure on goods and services, 1999 (as per cent of GNP)	18	Composition of Parliament (June 2002):	Seats:
Current government receipts, 1998 (as per cent of GNP)	40	Fianna Fail	81
General government debt, 2001 (as per cent of GNP)	44	Fine Gael	31
		Labour	21
		Progressive Democrats	8
		Green	6
		Socialist	1
		Sinn Fein	5
		Others	13
		Last general election: May 2002	

FOREIGN TRADE

Exports:		Imports:	
Exports of goods and services, as per cent of GNP (2001)	117	Imports of goods and services, as per cent of GNP (2001)	100
Main exports, 2001 (per cent of total):		Main imports, 2001 (per cent of total):	
Meat and meat preparation	2	Petroleum products	3
Dairy products	1	Chemicals and related products	12
Beverages	1	Textile manufacturing, clothing and footwear	3
Organic chemicals	14	Machinery and transport equipment	51
Medical and pharmaceutical products	7	*of which*:	
Machinery and transport equipment	45	Office machines	18
of which:		Electrical machinery	14
Office machines	27	Main suppliers, 2001 (per cent of total):	
Electrical machinery	11	United Kingdom	35
Main customers, 2001 (per cent of total):		Other European Union	23
United Kingdom	23	United States	15
Other European Union	38		
United States	17		

THE CURRENCY

Monetary unit: Euro	Currency unit per US dollar, average of daily figures:	
	Year 2002	0.94
	March 2003	1.08

1. Preliminary.

This Survey is published on the responsibility of the Economic *and* Development Review Committee *of the* OECD, *which is charged with the examination of the economic situation of* Member *countries.*

The economic situation and policies of Ireland *were reviewed by the* Committee *on* 14 April 2003. *The draft report was then revised in the light of the discussions and given final approval as the agreed report of the whole* Committee *on* 23 May 2003.

The Secretariat's draft report was prepared for the Committee by Hideyuki Ibaragi, Young-Sook Nam *and* Boris Cournède *under the supervision of* Yutaka Imai.

The previous Survey *of* Ireland *was issued in* June 2001.

Assessment and Recommendations

The Celtic Tiger era is over

The extraordinary growth in the second half of the 1990s, the era of the "Celtic Tiger", has given way to a more normal, albeit still rapid pace of expansion since 2001, though the extent of the slowdown has been more marked outside the multinationals sector. Some slackening in growth was in any case inevitable and even desirable given increased tensions in the economy, manifest in high inflation, worsening traffic congestion, rapidly rising house prices and recruitment difficulties. While the slowdown is closely linked to the burst of the ICT bubble, it also reflects a deterioration in Irish cost competitiveness. This has been due to strong inflation in the sheltered sector of the economy, reflecting the combined influence of large wage gains emanating from the tradables sector, low productivity growth in the sheltered sector and the generally expansionary effects of very low real interest rates since Ireland joined the European Monetary Union. The future trend growth over the medium term is now widely believed to be between 4 and 5 per cent for real GDP and a shade lower for GNP, a view shared by the OECD. The policy challenge facing the Irish economy in the immediate future is to ensure that both income expectations and public finances adjust to a slower growth environment. The former is necessary to guard against deterioration in international competitiveness, while the latter is required to ensure fiscal sustainability and the maintenance of a growth-supportive tax environment. Over a longer term, the broad aim of the authorities should be to ensure that the economy will continue to grow at a reasonably high rate and that policies will be more clearly oriented towards protecting interests of consumers rather than producers, notably through enhanced competition in service sectors.

The resilience of GDP masks the weakness of the national economy

At 6 per cent, real GDP growth was relatively well maintained in 2002, but in terms of real GNP, a measure not of domestic production but of national economic activity, growth was much weaker at well below 2 per cent. The wide gap between GDP and GNP that is accounted for by net factor income payments has been a consistent feature of the Irish economy, but a growth gap of over 4 per cent is unprecedented and attributable to a strong performance of the biomedical and pharmaceutical sectors where, margins are exceptionally high and accrue largely to foreign owners. The economy has lost momentum since late 2002 with a further slowdown in exports and a substantial weakening in business confidence. The demand for labour slackened throughout 2002, leading to a rise in the unemployment rate from its historical lows to 4.4 per cent in 2002, The current weak trend in activity is expected to prevail during 2003 but is forecast to give way to modest acceleration in 2004 on the assumed recovery of export markets. Construction activities are likely to remain a major source of buoyancy due to rapid development of the physical infrastructure and continued strong demand for housing.

The adjustment of income expectations to slower growth appears to be in progress

There are signs that adjustment in income expectations has begun to take hold. The recent central wage agreement of 7 per cent over the next eighteen months indicates that income expectations are adjusting to the new situation and will help to moderate inflation. The partnership process seems to have contributed to this outcome by promoting the common understanding of the emerging economic reality, even without a tax concession as offered by the government in the past. The new partnership agreement nonetheless included a series of special initiatives to deal with certain social issues. On the other hand, strong price pressures that prevail in the sheltered sector of the economy suggest that the adaptation of income expectations to slower growth still has some way to go. Inflation in the sheltered sector, however, could be expected to subside with wage moderation, though remaining higher than in the sector open to international competition. One reason for this projected inflation gap is the level adjustments to public sector wages following the benchmarking exercise, which put upward pressure on indirect taxes and public charges. It is important that future wage adjustment in the public sector should be strictly conditional upon the demonstration of higher efficiency.

... and so does the adjustment in public finances

The adjustment also appears to be taking place in public finances. The 2003 budget seems to be more consistent with slower underlying growth in the tax base than its two predecessors. Both the 2001 and 2002 budgets substantially overestimated revenues while underestimating spending pressures, which resulted in a worsening of the general government position from a surplus of 4.4 per cent of GDP in 2000 to an estimated deficit of 0.1 per cent in 2002. The error in the revenue projection was in part due to the reform of taxation which, despite its positive effects on economic incentives, made forecasting difficult. But it was also attributable to overestimation of Irish growth due to the unforeseen slowdown in global economic activity. The 2003 budget marks a departure from the earlier budgets in that it relies on increased taxation and allows a smaller increase in spending that is allocated selectively to priority areas. Even so, the general government deficit is projected to rise to 0.8 per cent of GDP in 2003.

But managing public spending and maintaining a supportive tax environment remains a longer-term challenge

The budget projections to 2005 in Ireland's latest Stability Programme Update envision the deficit continuing to rise to 1.2 per cent of GDP in the context of economic growth below potential. However, both the spending and revenue shares are projected to fall and the debt to GDP ratio to remain below 35 per cent. In the following decade, it will be necessary to exercise continued budget prudence so as to deal with spending pressures related to infrastructure development and a range of social services and to prepare further for the budgetary implications of population ageing. In an environment of less buoyant fiscal revenues, the need to clearly establish spending priorities and to ensure that value for money becomes the key criterion in all spending areas will become more important than ever.

Reforms to budget process and control should be intensified

To meet this challenge requires further significant improvements to the public expenditure management system. Despite some progress, further reforms to institutional arrangements will be needed to enhance aggregate spending control and strategic prioritisation. Among the most important is the adoption of a more top-down budgeting process and a rolling multi-annual budget "envelope" system. The move to a multi-annual framework for public investment is a positive step in this regard. Prioritisation of spending could also be facilitated by stepping up the ongoing efforts for systematic expenditure reviews, and by introducing sunset clauses to new programmes, which should help move resources away from those which no longer serve the original objectives.

The shift toward more flexible and results-focused budgeting and management should be stepped up

To enhance the efficiency of public service delivery, the government should accelerate its efforts to move from input-oriented management and budgeting toward one centred on outputs and outcomes. This will however need to be pursued in conjunction with strengthening accountability for results, which in turn requires developing more specific performance criteria and more effective monitoring and control systems. Routine and systematic evaluation and value-for-money audits should be in place in all spending areas. The government should also take steps to systematically integrate output indicators into the budgetary and policy-making process. Both *ex ante* indicators in the form of goals and *ex post* indicators as a means of verifying performance will need to be integrated to show the effectiveness of alternative programmes. In particular, it will be important to strengthen the role of the Parliament and the Comptroller and Auditor General in results-oriented auditing and reviewing control mechanisms. At the same time, the current efforts to develop the Management Information Framework (MIF) needs to be stepped up. Efficiency gains could also be made from reforms to human resource management in the public service including more open and competitive recruitment and performance-oriented personnel management practices. Given the limited progress made in this area in the past, it will be particularly important to develop the link between public sector pay increases and the modernisation of the public service, which was established in the new partnership agreement.

The use of market instruments in the public sector should be expanded

A more extensive use of market-based instruments such as contracting out, vouchers, internal contracts and benchmarking should help generate higher efficiency and better delivery of publicly funded services. In particular, there is still substantial scope for more use of user charges as a mean to contain cost pressures or reduce excessive demand. Water charges are a case in point. Ireland is unique among OECD countries in not charging domestic consumers for water services. A charging regime in this area could contribute to more efficient use of what is becoming an increasingly expensive resource. In addition, fees for higher education could be re-introduced. Several OECD countries have successfully targeted support for higher education through fees, loans and grant schemes which include provisions for the less well-off.

Funding of local governments could be better geared toward promoting the effectiveness of public expenditure

Improving the effectiveness of spending by sub-national governments should be a key element of public expenditure management reform. A wide-ranging programme of local government reform in recent years has greatly enhanced the quality of performance management system at local level. While pursuing the ongoing efforts to improve local accountability, reform should now aim at providing greater flexibility and decision making power to local authorities and increasing the share of funding which is locally levied. In this regard, serious consideration should be given to raising revenues by re-introducing local property taxes on residential housing, which has many advantages as a sub-national tax. The current grant system might be reformed to improve allocative and cost efficiency by moving towards block grants for those services which do not provide clear spillover effects and modifying the financing arrangements for earmarked grants to provide incentive to contain costs. There is also scope for streamlining sub-national public administration, given the plethora of local or regionally-based public bodies that operate outside local government. Efforts should also be made to enhance the level of co-ordination and co-operation between local authorities and between national/local authorities and other public service bodies to achieve effective planning and delivery of services.

Better planning and increased efficiency in infrastructure investment are necessary

Costs and benefits of public spending in several priority areas should be carefully considered. One such area is public infrastructure investment. The substantial increase in spending planned under the National Development Plan is justified to respond to the infrastructure needs resulting from strong economic growth in Ireland, in particular, in roads, public transport, and housing. But it is important to get the maximum mileage out of the increased spending. The final costs of the infrastructure investment under the National Development Plan are now envisaged to be much higher than initially planned. For example, the estimated costs of the national road programme had soared from € 5.9 billion in 1999 to € 15.8 billion in 2002, due mainly to construction cost inflation, design changes, additional land acquisition costs, and under-estimation of project prices. One way to overcome the constraints in the construction sector will be to accelerate the efforts to increase the import content of construction services, through such measures as further increasing the share of public procurement openly advertised internationally. The Government's intention to expand the involvement of the private sector in the funding and operation of the public infrastructure through Public Private Partnerships (PPP) is welcome in this regard, but in pursuing this strategy the appraisal procedures in place to determine that PPP is the best value option should be rigorously applied. In addition, contracts will need to be designed carefully to allow for an appropriate sharing of the risks associated with such major projects and emphasis will need to be placed on regulation and on providing the right frameworks and incentives.

The effectiveness of healthcare spending also needs to be improved

Another priority spending area is healthcare. Given the enormous increases in government expenditure on the health services and notwithstanding some real improvements in outputs, concerns remain about the efficiency and productivity of this sector. This is particularly manifest in public dissatisfaction about long waiting times for access to public hospitals, which seems to be exacerbated by a prevailing perception that people with private insurance jump the queue. To respond to the issue of access to care for public patients in public hospitals the regulations which limit the share of public beds occupied by private patients should be fully enforced. To better inform public perceptions and to improve decision making about priorities, greater transparency is required in relation to the existing distribution of resources within, and outputs of, the health services. More generally, the poorly developed information systems in the health sector hamper the measurement of performance, and priority should be given to accelerating efforts to improve the availability of relevant information. Enhancing the efficiency and effectiveness of health spending also requires comprehensive reforms to the organisation and management of the health sector. In particular, more co-ordination across the ambulatory sector and the inpatient care sector could help to achieve productivity gains and reduce the workload of hospitals. Serious consideration should be given to the proposals calling for a smaller number of health boards with improved governance structure, which would improve accountability and facilitate the rationalisation of service provision. Enhanced co-operation among health boards should be encouraged to reap the benefits from synergies and economies of scale. This would help to ensure consistent application of service and quality standards nation-wide.

Future prosperity will continue to depend on safeguarding competitiveness and remaining attractive to investment

Getting maximum value for money out of public spending will help to improve the quality of public services and to maintain the current tax environment. This is good for the citizen's welfare and for business development generally. It also helps Ireland to remain an attractive place for the foreign direct investment (FDI) that will continue to play a major role in the growth process. While Ireland's low-tax and other advantages such as English language and well-trained workers will continue to be positive features in attracting foreign investment, their merit is likely to diminish in relation to newly emerging competitors, particularly some of the candidate countries for EU accession. In addition, given the particularly strong response of productivity growth to FDI it would not be difficult for these countries to gain cost competitiveness quickly once the scale of FDI is increased. Faced with this challenge the authorities should at a minimum ensure that inflation in the sheltered sector does not undermine cost competitiveness given that the Irish price level converged to the average EU level and is now becoming among the highest in the region.

Inflation in the sheltered sector matters

Inflation in the sheltered sector of the economy matters for growth in several ways. *First*, it affects the cost competitiveness of the internationally traded sector to the extent that the services provided by the sheltered sector serve as inputs. *Second*, by raising the cost of living of workers it pushes up the wage claims in the internationally competing sector. *Third*, it influences inward migration that is likely to constitute an increasing source of labour force growth. The cost of housing is an important element of domestic inflation and needs to be reined in. The price of housing has been rising rapidly despite the increasing supply, and as more new houses have been built further away from the city centres the commuting time has lengthened and pressures on infrastructure have intensified. While roads and other physical infrastructure are being built within the framework of the National Development Plan, new forms of public transport such as the light rail system currently under construction in Dublin would alleviate the problem of commuting. In parallel, reform in urban planning regulations seems necessary to promote the housing capacity within the cities.

Progress in regulatory reform has been uneven and much remains to be done

Regulatory reform in the sheltered sector could contribute importantly to enhancing the growth prospect by weakening the pricing power of incumbents and boosting productivity. Good progress has been made in strengthening competitive forces in some areas such as telecommunications and taxis. Moreover, the Competition Authority has seen both its independence and resources substantially reinforced in line with the recommendations made by the OECD. In contrast, progress has been sluggish in most other areas, including pubs and legal and other professions, and further steps are necessary even in those areas where good progress has been made. In electricity, the creation of a power exchange would considerably promote the development of additional generating capacity by independent generators. This could and perhaps should be further encouraged by making an ownership separation between generation and transmission assets, and splitting the Electricity Supply Board's generating capacity into a number of competing units. In pharmacies, an arbitrary rule limiting the operation of pharmacists trained outside the country should be abolished. New initiatives to bring in more competition to land transport and airport operations are welcome, but they need to be followed through.

Strengthening focus on consumer interests not only enhances welfare but also helps the growth process

A key to future reform process, however, is the proposed National Policy Statement on Regulation that sets down the principles for the regulatory system. To mark a clear departure from the traditional policy focus on producer interests, the principles should anchor the regulatory system firmly in competition policy. There appears to be an increasing realisation among Irish people that the legacy of protecting producer interests in the sheltered sector at the expense of consumer interests is not only hurting their own welfare but also the competitiveness of the economy. The anti-inflation initiative in the new partnership agreement is a concrete manifestation of such a realisation. It is hoped that this initiative reinforces the role of the Competition Authority in fighting unhealthy pricing power in sectors where competitive forces are still inadequate.

The success in upgrading investment will depend on the availability of high-quality human capital

While safeguarding cost competitiveness helps, for a high income country like Ireland to continue to grow there is no escaping a shift in the supply structure towards higher value added. The authorities are now trying to promote higher value-added investment, through encouraging existing domestic and foreign companies to engage in knowledge-intensive activities and by inviting innovation-oriented new FDI. Given the large-scale presence of high-tech foreign companies, there appear to exist some economies of agglomeration, as illustrated by successful cases of domestic venture start-ups and diversification of activities by multinationals, notably in Dublin. The success of the strategy of upgrading business activity will, however, depend importantly on how many high-skilled workers and researchers Ireland can provide or attract.

... that can be increased by the reform of the innovation system and education and training

With the rapidly upgrading skill requirements, higher education institutions now face the challenges to increase enrolment and retention rates, to maintain high standards of teaching and to further develop research capability. Research and development activities at the universities are being strengthened by the unprecedented increase in the funding for research, which needs to be allocated based on competitive evaluation by a third party. In addition, more systematic efforts will be needed to address the weaknesses in technology transfer and commercialisation of research results through an improved co-operation between businesses and higher education institutions, while ensuring competition between different consortia. Emphasis has also been placed on improving human capital at work, by encouraging lifelong learning and business investment in training, for example through the "skillnets" initiative. Flexible arrangements are being introduced to allow employed early school-leavers to obtain certificates on a part-time basis. The increased number of mature age students seeking learning opportunities could be accommodated more effectively by introducing flexibility into the traditionally rigid system of student selection and administration in higher education institutions.

Growth should also be environmentally sustainable

Continuing economic growth should also be environmentally sustainable. Achievement of this objective is being aided by the increasing use of economic instruments. Carbon taxation is being considered to reduce greenhouse gas emissions and would be a step forward, provided that tax rates are uniform across all sectors and in line with expected prices for EU emission permits. The peat industry should not be exempt from such taxation. Waste management is also moving in the right direction with the introduction of a landfill tax, weight-based charges for households and use of producer responsibility levies. Taxes and levies should, however, be soundly anchored to measured externalities and should not be used to meet arbitrary targets. While there is no shortage of water and clean rivers, water quality has deteriorated. There seems no reason to continue to finance household water supplies and waste water treatment from general taxation. The main environmental problem, seen as excess nutrient content in rivers, will be addressed in the context of the development of a national action programme to give effect to the Nitrates and other Directives. This effort should include the use of economic instruments.

In conclusion

Having slowed down sharply, the Irish economy is now faced with the challenge of securing the basis for future growth. Income expectations seem to be adjusting to the new reality, and so does the 2003 budget. Yet difficult tasks remain in safeguarding cost competitiveness, moving up the value chain, securing sound public finances, ensuring value for money in public services and making growth environmentally sustainable. Safeguarding cost competitiveness and enhancing welfare require new initiatives to contain housing prices as well as stepped-up reform efforts in much of the sheltered sector of the economy, including the public sector, which affects prices through both taxation and public charges. Fiscal policy needs to guard against complacency, and to move back towards balance, or a surplus if circumstances require, over the medium-term, while focussing on improving the structure of the economy. To maintain a growth-friendly tax environment and ensure fiscal sustainability, it is essential to further improve the management of public expenditure by: harnessing an output orientation and top-down approach in budgeting; assessing projects on their relative merits; giving local governments both greater freedom and responsibility in decision making; and taking advantage of market mechanisms in some appropriate areas of the provision of merit goods. To break away for good from the legacy of protecting producer interests, the National Policy Statement on Regulation should establish principles for the regulatory system that are firmly based on the idea of promoting competition. Linked to this, the high value-added orientation of business investment strategy requires enhanced quality of human capital and capacity for innovation, the efficient provision of which is most likely achieved through a system where competition plays an important role. In sum, with the Irish economy moving to a rather slower growth path than in the second half of the 1990s, both income expectations and public finances are having to adjust. But taking full advantage of Ireland's growth potential requires a range of structural reforms, in both the public and the private sectors, to create a more competitive environment and contribute to continuing prosperity and enhanced welfare.

I. Adjusting to slower growth and ensuring prosperity

The nature of the growth slowdown

Ireland's remarkable growth performance that began from the mid-1990s and continued into the start of the new millennium has led to rapid convergence of productivity levels towards the EU average, while employment growth has also been exceptionally strong. Living standards have increased dramatically as a result. Between 1995 and 2000 real GDP grew by an annual average of nearly 10 per cent. It slowed sharply in 2001 to 5.7 per cent but is estimated to have grown at about the same rate in 2002. The resilience in terms of GDP is in marked contrast to the sharper slowdown evident in terms of GNP, which is estimated to have slowed to below 2 per cent in 2002 from 4.6 per cent in 2001 and a high of 10.7 per cent in 2000 (Figure 1). This reflects a continued expansion of the large multinational sector operating in Ireland.[1]

Growth since the mid-1990s had been clearly above the economy's potential growth rate, though it is difficult to measure this given the endogenous nature of both productivity and labour supply. The Irish population structure in the 1990s has been unusually favourable in increasing labour supply. The expansion in the labour force has been much greater than in the rest of the EU, reflecting different demographic circumstances; namely rising female participation rates, inflows of migration, a high rate of natural increase and a corresponding reduction in age dependency (Figures 2 and 6). But the available pool of labour that existed at the start of the 1990s has effectively been exhausted as the Irish economy moved to full employment levels in recent years. The unemployment rate fell from as high as 15.7 per cent in April 1993 to a low of 3.7 per cent in the first half of 2001, which led to increased recruitment difficulties.

Above potential growth has also resulted in growing infrastructure pressures as evidenced by rapid house price increases, congestion and longer commuting times, particularly in Dublin.[2] Competitiveness has been reduced by price and wage inflation, which has been reinforced by infrastructure constraints. Given these considerations, growth has had to slow sooner or later even though the shift down in Irish economic growth has been undoubtedly linked to internationally

Figure 1. **Growth in GDP and GNP: the widening gap**
Per cent change

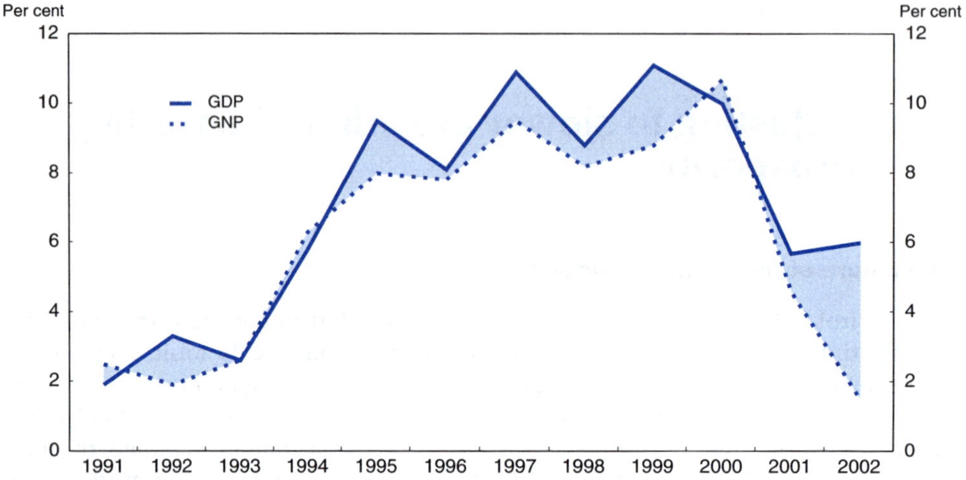

Source: Central Statistics Office.

Figure 2. **Irish labour force growth**
Annual per cent change

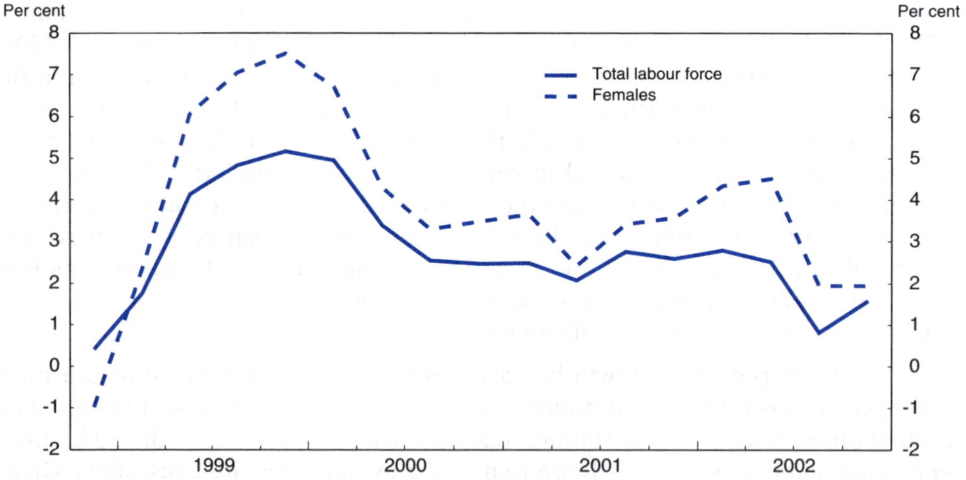

Source: Central Statistics Office.

weak FDI flows that fed into a fall in the number of employed in the multinational companies, particularly in the ICT sector.

The apparent resilience of economic activity is, however, somewhat surprising given the series of economic shocks that affected the Irish economy between mid-2000 and 2002. Dependence on foreign direct investment (FDI), especially in high-tech sectors originating in the United States, meant that Ireland was particularly exposed to the slowdown in the technology sector from mid-2000. Furthermore, the foot and mouth disease scare and the containment measures invoked curtailed domestic activity in the first half of 2001. The slowdown in world economic activity in the wake of the September 11 terrorist attacks, corporate accounting scandals and the on-going threat of war throughout 2002 suggested that an open-economy like Ireland's would have been expected to experience a much pronounced slowdown in economic activity. The diversification in FDI investment in recent years would seem to have helped buffer Ireland's growth performance from the full impact of these shocks. While sectors like ICT, tourism and agri-food took the brunt of the shocks, biomedical and pharmaceutical sectors continued to perform strongly in the difficult global trading environments.[3] As well, while machinery and equipment investment weakened sharply, housing construction and public investment, mainly in road building, has remained quite strong. The continued expansion of public investment associated with the implementation of the National Development Plan, together with the large scale of hiring by the public sector, suggests that fiscal policy was expansionary.

A persistent and widening gap between GDP (a measure of all economic activity in Ireland) and GNP (a measure of activity by Irish nationals) is an important feature of the Irish economy that has depended heavily on foreign direct investment. The gap corresponds to net factor income payments, mostly profits accruing to foreign companies operating in Ireland. It has increased from 4 per cent of GDP in 1980 to 11.4 per cent in 1990, and further to an estimated 19.8 per cent in 2002. As Figure 1 shows, the gap can be volatile, reflecting a large fluctuation in the composition of production by sectors that are rather narrowly-based and have varying profit margins (see Annex III).

The demand for labour throughout the economy has begun to slacken over the last eighteen months. The unemployment rate began to rise from its historical lows to some 4.4 per cent in 2002. The rebound in the unemployment rate has not been as substantial as might have been expected, partly because of the strong growth in public sector jobs. The muted rise in unemployment may also reflect labour hoarding following the shortages and recruitment difficulties of recent years. Employment in the private sector, however, has ceased to grow.

Labour force growth slowed significantly during 2002. Even the rise in female participation rates slowed during 2002. Somewhat contrary to expectations, given cost of living increases and the rapid increase in house prices, migration flows into Ireland have remained strong with the net inflow into the country reaching 28 800 in the year to April 2002 (the latest available data), up from 26 300 a year earlier (Figure 3). These high migration flows could reflect the more pronounced slowdown in other economies making Ireland still attractive for relocation.

In the face of the slowdown in activity from the highs of the 1990s, inflation remains the highest in the euro area, reflecting rapid price increases in the non-traded sectors of the economy, particularly services. Having remained low for much of the exceptional growth phase, higher inflation appeared to become more entrenched throughout 2001 and 2002 (Figure 4). Although the impact of some one-off factors from 2001 has worn off, the inflation rate in 2002 remained persistently high due mainly to non-traded service inflation. One important factor behind the high service price inflation is a rapid rise in housing prices, which affected inflation both directly through greater interest payments and indirectly through larger wage claims.

Despite concerns about a possible bubble, housing price increases slowed in 2001, partly as a result of the strong supply response with another new peak being set for house completions. Having increased stamp duties and removed mortgage interest deductibility against rental income in recent years, the authorities reversed these measures in the 2002 budget, which provided a boost

Figure 3. **Immigration**
Net immigration, thousands

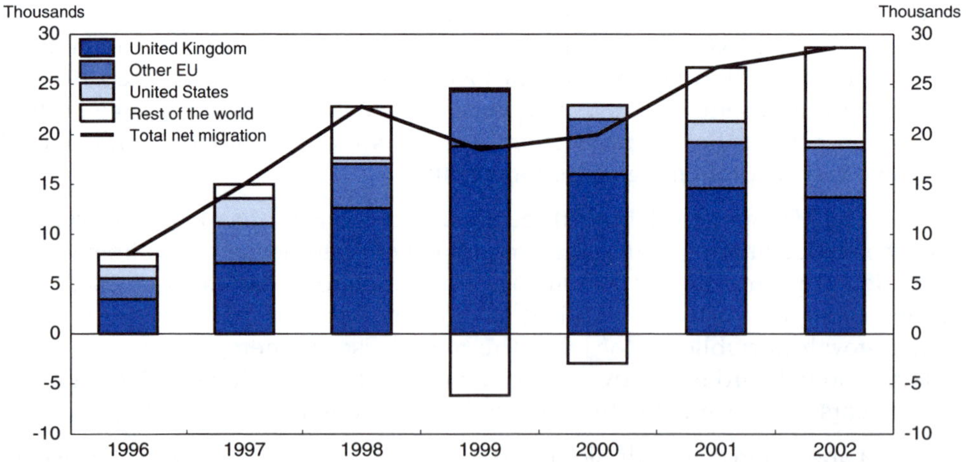

Source: Central Statistics Office.

Figure 4. **Indicators of inflation**
Per cent change over 12 months

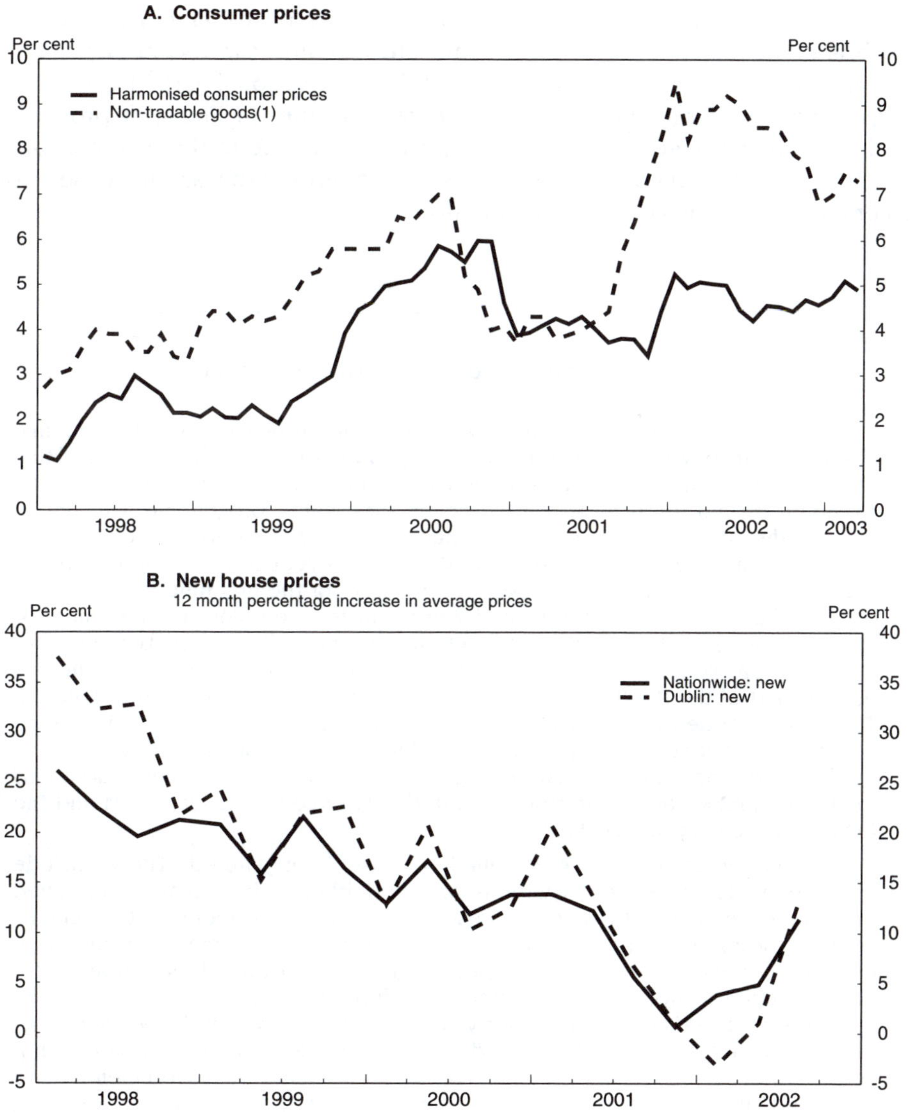

1. Non-tradable goods reflect only prices for services. The non-tradable price index is distorted downwards in November 2000 when the treatment of child services, health insurance and tuition fees was altered.

Source: Central Statistics Office.

for the housing market. As a consequence both investors and first-time buyers returned to the market and strong house price growth resumed. There is, however, no strong evidence to suggest that the current situation in the housing market should be characterised as a bubble (Duffy, 2002).

Along with a continuing easing of pressures in the labour market, wage growth is expected to slow from the high rates recorded in recent years. Slower wage growth is consistent with the terms of the new national agreement *Sustaining Progress* (see Box 1) recommending pay increases more in line with productivity developments. However, the loss of competitiveness due to the recent appreciation of the euro may mean that even these more moderate wage increases would further undermine the competitive situation.

Box 1. The new partnership agreement

Under the new *Sustaining Progress* agreement the proposals cover a wide range of areas, from pay rates in the public and private sectors to initiatives tackling affordable housing, social inclusion and inequality. The pay increases cover an 18-month period, until mid-2004. However, the overall programme will run for 3 years, the same as previous social partnership agreements. Under the new agreement the overall pay increase would be 7 per cent over 18 months. Private sector employees would get a 3 per cent increase for the first nine months, 2 per cent for the following six months and 2 per cent for the following three months. Those employed in the public sector get the same overall increase, but only after a 6-month pay pause. The public sector employees will also benefit from the pay rises as part of the Public Sector Benchmarking process (see Box 4 in Chapter II). This recommended pay awards ranging between 2 and 25 per cent with an average of 8.9 per cent. The payment of the Benchmarking awards applying to the public sector under the new national agreement would be 25 per cent backdated to December 2001 at the start of the period, 50 per cent in January 2004 and the final 25 per cent by mid 2005.

A number of non-pay elements have also been agreed. These include enhanced statutory redundancy terms, an affordable housing initiative, improved procedures to deal with union representation and a requirement that unions accept binding arbitration when disputes arise in certain areas. The new programme also includes a series of special initiatives to provide social and economic progress subject to budgetary affordability. At present these include insurance costs, housing, child poverty, waste management, childcare, unemployment, educational disadvantage and drug abuse. In addition, the new partnership agreement has recommended that a group comprising of Government, trade union and employer representatives be set up to identify the causes of worsening inflation in the Irish economy and to recommend strategies to deter unwarranted price rises (see Annex I).

Future prospects

Short-term outlook

After showing remarkable resilience up to the third quarter of 2002, the economy seems to have lost momentum as exports slowed and business confidence weakened substantially. The recent Purchasing Managers' Index for manufactures shows a contraction in March 2003 for the sixth consecutive month. This weak trend, accompanied by falling business fixed investment, is likely to prevail during most of 2003 under the combined influence of a slowdown in the growth of Irish export markets and the appreciation of the euro during 2002 and into 2003[4] (Figure 5). But with world economic growth recovering and the negative impact of the earlier appreciation of the euro fading, Irish GDP is forecast to pick up speed from 3¼ per cent in 2003 to about 4¼ per cent in 2004 (Table 1).

The components of domestic demand underpinning growth throughout the forecast period are housing investment, which is aided by very low real interest rates and favourable tax treatment, and public investment, which continues to increase to make up for insufficient infrastructure. The underlying impact of budgetary changes is slightly contractionary in 2003 and slightly expansionary in 2004[5] (see Chapter II). But given the large margin of error surrounding such estimates, it would be more appropriate to consider the fiscal stance to be roughly neutral during the forecast period.

Labour market conditions are expected to weaken further. With public sector recruitment coming to a halt, employment growth is forecast to decelerate further in 2003 before rebounding somewhat in 2004. It nonetheless remains below the growth of the labour force, so that the unemployment rate is likely to edge up. The weak prospect for the labour market has resulted in wage moderation. As noted above, the recent central wage agreement implies private sector wage growth to be about 5 per cent in 2003 and 4½ per cent in 2004.

Reflecting wage moderation and the impact of the euro appreciation, inflation is forecast to come down, though one-off measures from the 2003 budget and a series of public service and other administered price rises are likely to attenuate the downslide in 2003. The HICP inflation is hence forecast to slow down from 4¾ per cent in 2002 to only 4¼ per cent in 2003 before decelerating more distinctly in 2004.

Longer-term prospects

Long-term prospects for the Irish economy remain broadly favourable. Some of the structural forces underlying the economy's recent slowdown remain of great importance when examining its future prospects and in particular when calculating the economy's potential growth rate. These include the prospects for

Figure 5. **Exchange rate and unit labour costs**

1991 = 100

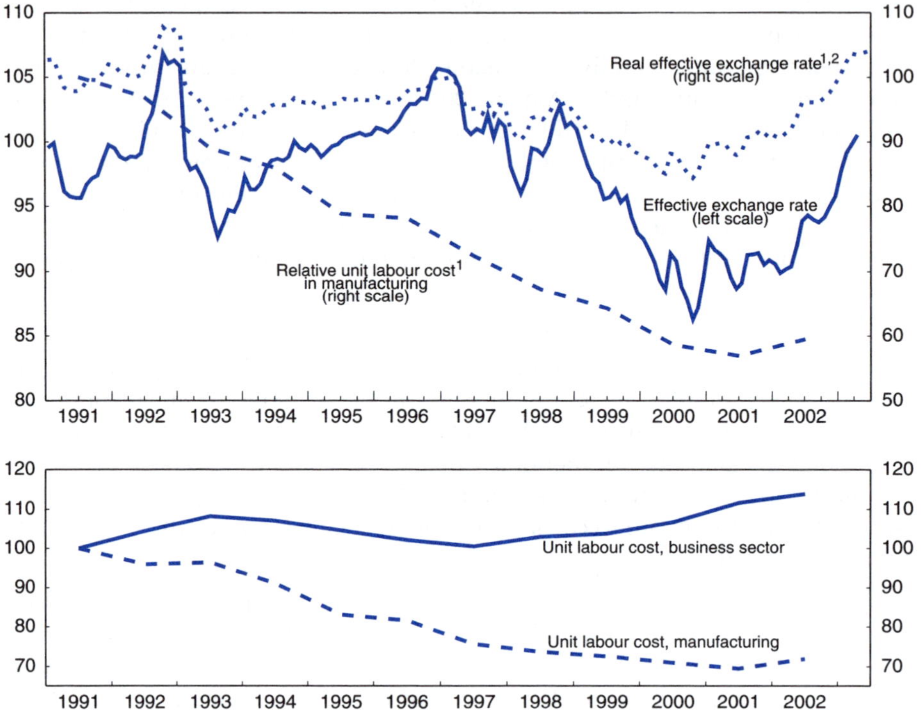

1. Vis-à-vis forty-one countries.
2. Using consumer price index.
Source: OECD.

business investment, for responding to the economy's infrastructural constraints and for future labour force growth.

Business investment grew rapidly in the 1990s. As a result, the growth rate of capital stock roughly doubled to about 5 per cent in the second half of the past decade, contributing to the growth of potential output. At the same time, capital productivity continued to increase at a diminishing pace and its level has begun to fall since two years ago. Prospects for business investment will depend on the extent to which regulatory reform opens up latent business opportunities domestically and Ireland remains an attractive place for FDI.

While prospects for FDI inflows depend importantly on the recovery of the global FDI flows generally and in particular of the activity in technology

Table 1. **Short-term outlook**

	1999 current prices % GDP	2001	2002	2003	2004
Private consumption	48.1	5.0	2.5	3.0	3.5
Government consumption	13.9	10.5	8.7	1.5	0.7
Gross fixed investment	23.7	1.0	–0.7	–0.2	2.1
Construction	14.5	4.5	2.0	2.0	2.5
Machinery and equipment	9.2	–3.0	–4.0	–3.0	1.5
Final domestic demand	85.8	4.9	2.8	2.0	2.7
Stockbuilding[1]	0.5	–0.4	–0.2	0.2	0.1
Total domestic demand	86.3	4.4	2.5	2.2	2.7
Exports of goods and services	88.0	6.7	4.9	3.5	7.1
Imports of goods and services	74.2	6.1	1.8	3.0	6.5
Foreign balance[1]	13.8	1.6	3.6	1.1	1.8
GDP at constant prices		6.0	6.0	3.2	4.2
GNP at constant prices		4.9	1.5	2.1	3.1
GDP price deflator		5.3	4.9	4.0	3.6
GDP at current prices	100.0	11.6	11.2	7.3	8.0
Memorandum item:					
Private consumption deflator		4.2	4.8	4.2	3.2
Consumer price index harmonised		4.0	4.7	4.1	3.2
Underlying price index harmonised		4.5	5.2	4.2	3.2
Potential output whole economy		7.0	6.2	5.7	5.4
Output gap whole economy		5.8	5.7	3.2	2.1

1. Contribution to GDP growth.
Source: OECD.

sectors, one of the major threats to inward FDI in Ireland in the medium term is the expansion of the EU to the east (Barry and Hannon, 2001). Over the course of the 1990's the inward stock of FDI in the ten applicant countries increased 23-fold (albeit mainly from Europe itself). Most of this was "market seeking" rather than attempting to integrate production into EU production networks, as is the case in Ireland. Therefore, up to now, this type of FDI has not posed a direct threat to Ireland. With the accession of these countries, competition with Ireland will become more and more direct. Ireland will encounter competition on many of the factors that have made it attractive for FDI in the past such as low corporation tax regime; the skill levels of the workforce; cost competitiveness; and certainty of overall policy environment. Moreover, these countries have the advantage of a higher degree of centrality to the core EU market compared to Ireland.

The rapid improvement in infrastructure and the skill levels accumulated should, however, help Ireland to maintain its status as an attractive location for future FDI flows. Moreover, there is already a critical mass of existing FDI that should have a positive demonstration effect on potential FDI inflows.[6] The enlargement of the EU is also likely to increase total FDI flows substantially so that a more competitive environment for FDI may not represent a zero-sum game for

Ireland. Although Ireland may receive a lower share of investment flows, the level of inflows to Ireland may well be maintained.

The so-called infrastructure deficit should become a less important factor determining potential growth as the economy shifts to a more normal growth path. In addition, such constraints are rapidly being dealt with through the implementation of the infrastructure investment programme under the National Development Plan (see Chapter III). Improved economic infrastructure should affect potential output through both productivity and labour supply. It should raise productivity both directly by reducing bottlenecks and indirectly by inducing more FDI inflows. It should also increase labour supply by helping to raise the participation of second income earners as well as by facilitating immigration. In practice, it is difficult to disentangle these different effects (Denny and Guiomard, 1997).[7] In the Irish context, various positive effects of infrastructure investment on the economy emanate from its impact on the housing market as it increases the supply of serviced land and facilitates commuting.

Labour supply over the period to 2010 will continue to benefit from the comparatively favourable natural increase in working age population, while the participation rate could rise only slightly. Immigration flows are also likely to remain an important source of the labour force growth, even though they will be influenced by higher costs of living, reduced growth of job opportunities and a change in related labour market policies (Figure 6).

The cost of living will remain high as long as Ireland enjoys above EU average growth, even though its rate of increase should moderate. An important component of the cost of living is the price of housing. The 2003 budget contained a number of measures that will affect the housing market going forward.[8] In particular, the cost of new houses now reflects the increase in VAT from 12.5 per cent to 13.5 per cent. On the other hand, the recent Planning and Development Amendment Act 2002 should serve to boost supply.[9] Although demand has moderated, demographic factors alone are expected to underpin the housing market going forward. The Economic and Social Research Institute estimates that there is a need for over 40 000 dwelling on an annual basis between 2001 and 2006.[10] The supply response and policy changes should moderate the rapid price increase of recent years, though it is unlikely that house prices will fall in the short term.

More generally, although some convergence towards euro area inflation rates is expected to occur, the Irish cost of living is likely to increase faster for some time. To a significant extent this is an unavoidable consequence of the dualistic pattern of growth with the traded sectors of the economy setting the pace for wage increases commensurate with their large productivity gains, which result in higher inflation in the non-traded sectors where productivity improvement is more limited.

Figure 6. **Decomposition of growth in labour supply**
Contribution to growth

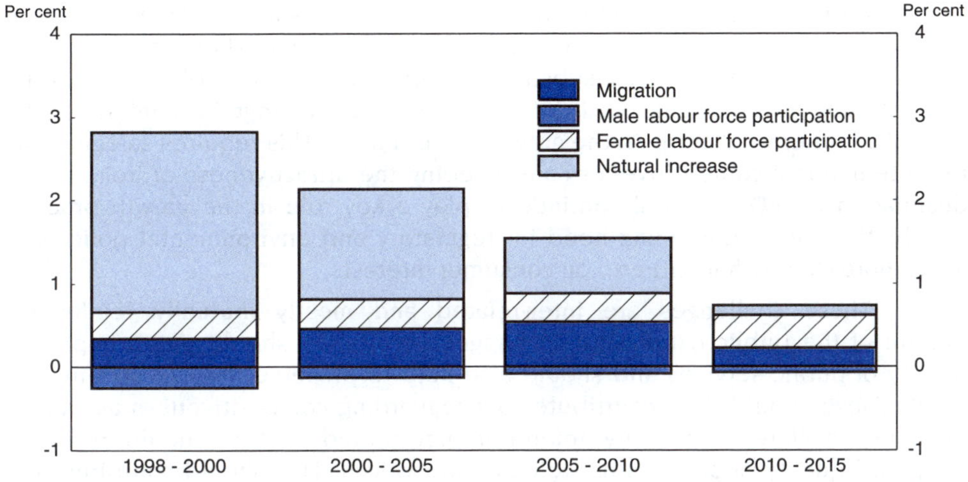

Source: ESRI.

The growth in the number of jobs available to immigrants will also be much reduced, and policy has switched to limiting inflows from low-income countries and encouraging immigrants with high skills in selected areas of shortage (see Chapter IV). Nevertheless, the prospects for the rest of the current decade still remain favourable.

To sum up, the Irish economy is operating at, or close to, full employment and participation rates are now close to the EU average, placing the focus squarely on underlying productivity as the key determinant of the potential growth rate. Average productivity growth is forecast to decline slightly as high-technology industries mature and the economy continues to become more services intensive. In the central scenario, productivity as measured by GDP per worker is assumed to grow by 3½ per cent per year, and the labour supply by 1½ per cent with the natural increase and immigration contributing roughly evenly[11]. Hence a growth of potential GDP of 5 per cent is assumed. Furthermore, the gap between GDP and GNP is estimated to continue to widen albeit slightly. This is based on the assumption that net FDI inflow will remain broadly unchanged and that the resulting fall in the growth rate of foreign-owned capital stock will be less than entirely offset by an increase in the rate of return. The potential growth rates of GDP and GNP will nonetheless continue to depend heavily on both the level of FDI inflow as well as its profitability (see Annex III).

Policy challenges

The challenges that the prospective situation presents for economic policy are multiple. First, there is a major task for public finances to adjust to the slower growth environment so that their soundness is assured. This means reconciling continuing large demands on public spending with smaller increases in tax revenues, which necessitates substantial improvement in public expenditure management system (Callan *et al.* 2002). The second challenge is to minimise the risks of a further weakening in the growth performance. This requires safeguarding the international competitiveness and keeping the attractiveness of Ireland as a destination for FDI that will continue to play a key role in the growth process. Finally, there is a compelling need for regulatory and environmental policies to focus more clearly than hitherto on consumer interests.

These challenges are inter-related and mostly mutually reinforcing. Reform of the public expenditure management system should entail improved quality of public services and should also help to preserve the low tax environment. These should then contribute to safeguarding competitiveness as well as enhanced welfare. Regulatory reform in non-traded sectors should result in improved quality of services as well as lower prices. This should contribute not only to better welfare but also to improved growth prospects by limiting deterioration in cost competitiveness and supporting labour force growth. In what follows, Chapters II and III address the public finance challenge, whereas the competitiveness and welfare challenges are mainly dealt with in Chapter IV.

The challenge for public finances

During the period of extraordinary economic expansion tax revenues consistently overshot budget estimates by large margins. This more than covered spending overruns that averaged about ½ per cent of GNP and facilitated the reform of taxation and benefit systems that improved incentives to work. But in the last two years, with growth slowing, revenue shortfalls emerged, while expenditures gradually adjusted. The 2003 budget appears to be better adapted to the slower growth environment, once offsetting revenue and spending measures are taken into account. That budget, while allowing for only a small rise in the overall envelope, increased spending in key priority areas of infrastructure, health, education and social welfare.

Difficulty in reconciling revenue and expenditure growth will be compounded in the coming years by significant spending pressures. These include the National Development Plan, Public Sector Benchmarking, the Health strategy and a range of social provision actions underway as part of the partnership agreements. The budget projections to 2005 contained in the latest Stability Programme Update nonetheless indicate that public finance positions are likely to remain broadly healthy with the gross debt to GDP ratio remaining below 35 per cent on the basis of a small rise in the deficit in the context of below-potential growth. The sensitivity analysis carried out in the same context, however, shows that the budget balance is relatively responsive to a change in GDP growth. Looking forward, the impact of the ageing of population will start to bear on public spending after 2005, even though the pace of population ageing is slower than in many other European countries. It would therefore be necessary to exercise continued budget prudence beyond 2005 to deal with spending pressures that ensue.

To keep public spending under control in a sustainable manner it is necessary to go beyond setting, and monitoring the adherence to, cash limits to spending. It is a major task requiring spending allocation based on the evaluation of output or results of each programme, reassessment of fiscal relations between levels of government, and reform of the system of service provision, including the delineation of the role of the private sector.

Ensuring prosperity

In order to ensure continued prosperity it is necessary to maintain competitiveness given the importance of Ireland remaining an effective export platform. As noted above, the increase in prices in the non-traded sectors of the economy has been quite pronounced in recent years. The cost base of this sector is substantially determined by wage growth, which has been experiencing very high rates by international standards in recent years. Higher prices in the non-traded sectors also increase the cost base for the traded sectors of the economy. The traded sector cannot easily pass on higher costs to the world through higher prices, so that profitability of firms in this sector risks to be curtailed, potentially leading to retrenchment in their operations and job losses. The rising cost of living in the economy is also likely to reduce the attractiveness of Ireland as a location for high value-added investment and associated high-skill workers. While inflationary forces may be moderating in the shorter term, the international environment is in a historically low inflation environment so that higher relative inflation will be Ireland's main threat to growth.

The role of the centrally agreed wage accord in the inflation process has not been obvious. The social partnership has nonetheless likely helped to promote a common understanding of the problems facing the country and contributed to industrial peace. Moderate rates of wage growth agreed between the social partners, in exchange for tax cuts, appear to have been exceeded by actual wage increases by a significant margin (see Annex II). This process of setting a wage norm might become more relevant in a lower growth environment in coming to a shared view of what the economy can afford. But actual wage determination will continue to depend on the particular situation of a specific industry or a company. In these circumstances, excessive wage claims would seem more likely to be accommodated in those sectors that are sheltered from competitive pressures as higher costs can be more easily shifted to prices.

Promoting competition, particularly in the sheltered sectors of the economy, through improving the regulatory environment can therefore contribute significantly to containing cost pressures. Ireland has had some success in introducing competition in certain sectors. Deregulation in the telecommunications and aviation sectors has shown the gains that can result from increased competition. Considerable restructuring and change have taken place as incumbents sought to improve efficiency and as the new entrants sought to get a foothold in markets. Ultimately such competition has yielded more choice, improved services, and lower prices for consumers. Progress has also been made in substantially strengthening the power of the competition authority, and new reform initiatives have been taken in the energy and land transport sectors, as well as in professions. The success in pursuing reforms in the sheltered sectors of the economy will be key to safeguarding cost competitiveness.

Ensuring prosperity for an Ireland that has already caught up with EU average income levels and is losing cost competitiveness requires a continued shift in the economic structure towards higher value added activities. From this perspective the Industrial Development Authority (IDA), which has been instrumental in attracting FDI to Ireland, has recently changed its focus towards investment that is higher value added and requires high skill levels. As well, Enterprise Ireland has encouraged similar changes among indigenous companies. Their stated strategy is to promote investments that are innovation rather than production oriented, and which provide a better link to an increasingly sophisticated business environment. Economic activities with these kinds of characteristics may justify higher wage levels and so allow Ireland to maintain economic growth in the absence of a strong labour surplus it has had until recently. This strategy, however, necessitates greater efforts in upgrading the skill levels of Irish workers as well as research capacity.

Enhancing welfare

Ireland still suffers from the legacy of policy that was oriented towards protecting producers' interests at the expense of consumers' welfare. That consumer interests are only weakly represented in the social partnership process is telling in this respect. A challenge for policy is to dismantle this legacy. Many of the regulatory reform initiatives currently underway should put consumers' welfare at their central focus. The National Policy Statement on Regulation, which is currently under preparation, should set out principles that should anchor the regulatory system firmly in competition policy.

That legacy can also be detected in environmental policy, where interests of producers of pollution, be they firms or households, are sometimes protected.

Ireland has adopted a promising policy approach, including the extensive use of economic instruments, in many areas of environmental protection. But weak resolve of policymakers in fighting special interests and insufficient advocacy activities have raised the costs of compliance born by the rest of the economy. Notable examples include continued use of peat in power generation, non-charging of water use by households, and the absence of taxation of excessive fertiliser application.

II. Consolidating the public finances

Gradual adjustment of public finances to slower growth

The public finance position has deteriorated markedly from the period of large surpluses recorded in the late 1990s and 2000. The slowdown in the economy in 2001 and 2002, particularly in real GNP, which may better reflect the economy's base for income and taxation purposes, has led to lower revenue growth, while spending continued to expand at a high pace. The public finance out-turns for 2002 showed the general government balance moving into a small deficit (see Figure 7).

In recent years forecasting public finance out-turns has become particularly difficult mainly on the revenue side. The benign state of the public finances

Figure 7. **Evolution of Irish public finance**
Per cent of GDP

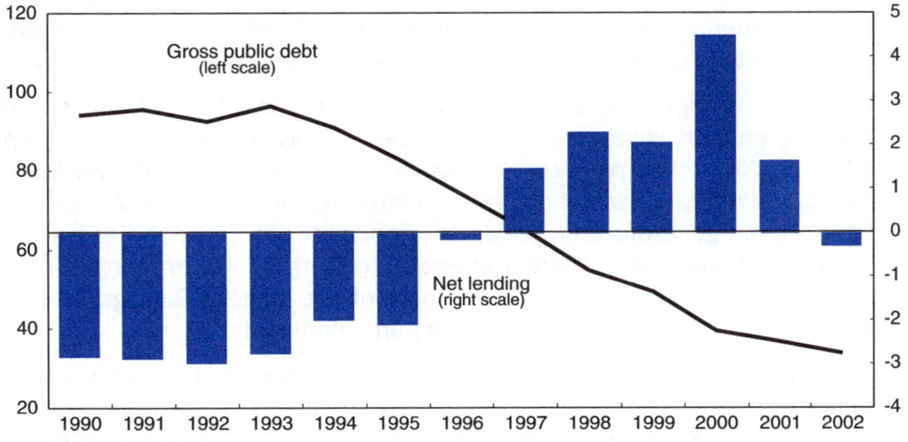

1. OECD preliminary estimates for 2002.
Source: OECD.

in the high growth era facilitated substantial changes to the tax parameters, and this has added potential sources of forecast error during the on-going transition period. Significant recent changes include the introduction of a system of tax credits, individualisation, harmonisation of corporation tax rates and a move to a calendar tax year. There was an additional difficulty of forecasting economic growth in an increasingly uncertain global environment. On the expenditure side, on the other hand, while there was a non-negligible over-run in 2001, spending was contained within budget in 2002.

The preparation of the 2001 budget was based on the assumption of continued high growth. The entire package of tax cuts and expenditure increases was assessed at that time to be roughly neutral by the OECD (OECD, 2001) or expansionary by at least 0.5 per cent of GDP by the European Union (Council Opinion on the 2000 the Stability Programme). The pertinent question was whether any injection of fiscal stimulus was appropriate for the Irish economy at that juncture. This was the main concern of the European Union, and its dispute with the Irish authorities revolved around the fundamental uncertainty about what economic stage Ireland was at.

The 2001 budget, however, introduced a special savings incentive scheme that could have a dampening effect on inflationary pressures present in the overheating economy at the time, even though the primary objective of this measure was to encourage people to save a larger part of their disposable income in the longer term to partially redress the problem of undersaving for retirement and other foreseeable contingencies (see Box 2 for a description of this scheme and its take-up and possible cost to the Exchequer out to 2007). It however remains to be seen to what extent the scheme has reached the objective, that is, encouraging more savings in the economy, while costs to the Exchequer could be large. This is because of non-negligible probability that individuals switch savings from other saving instruments to the new scheme rather than actually saving additionally.

The 2002 budget was aiming at providing a modest fiscal stimulus to the economy. The general government surplus was forecast to decline from 1.4 per cent of GDP in 2001 to 0.7 per cent in 2002. But there was a marked slowdown in projected tax revenue growth, and the expenditure measures announced were considerably more generous than previously anticipated. Total spending was forecast to rise by 11.6 per cent. Current spending undershot, but undershooting of revenues was greater. The depressing impact of the Special Savings Incentive Accounts (SSIAs) on income tax receipts was particularly notable.

The 2003 budget marked a return to a more orthodox mix of tax increase and spending growth restraint. The downward revisions in forecast economic growth has meant that, unlike previous years, it was no longer possible to increase expenditure while at the same time reducing tax rates. The budget outlined a number of additional spending initiatives to those contained in the annual Public

Box 2. Special savings incentive scheme

Under the terms of the scheme, for every amount saved in a special savings incentive account (SSIA), an additional 25 per cent is contributed by the Exchequer to the account. Account holders must be over the age of 18 and can only open a single SSIA. Participants in the scheme must commit to save a certain amount each month for a period of five years. The minimum monthly payment is € 12.70 and the maximum is € 253.95. The monthly contributions are fixed for the first twelve months, but thereafter, the individual can save any amount in this range for the remaining 4 years. The cash is credited each month by the Exchequer directly to the SSIA. However, if there is an early withdrawal from an SSIA, the full amount withdrawn will suffer tax at the rate of 23 per cent.

The scheme has been very popular with over 1.17 million accounts opened before the deadline of April 2002. Between its inception in May and year-end 2001, the scheme is estimated to have cost the Exchequer over € 70 million. In 2002, the cost is estimated to have been nearly € 430 million with a large number of new accounts opened prior to the April deadline. Based on the level of contributions for the first year, which under the terms of the scheme are fixed, the Exchequer is exposed to over € 500 million top-up contributions in full year costs. However, after the first year of the scheme each individual can increase or decrease their contributions. Rates of return on contributions, however, get higher and higher as the scheme approaches the end of its five years. If an increase sufficiently outweighs the inevitable attrition from the scheme, then the government's exposure could be much higher. If all account holders were to survive and increase their contributions to the ceiling, then the maximum cost to the Exchequer would be close to € 900 million (some 0.7 per cent of GDP).

Services Spending Estimates, concentrated in the areas of social welfare, public sector pay and transport infrastructure. These expenditures are largely financed out of a series of increased indirect taxation changes. In contrast to recent years, the changes in direct taxation were very modest. The main measures contained in Budget 2003 are outlined in Box 3.

The overall impact of the Budget package of tax rises and expenditure increases might be mildly contractionary this year, though any judgement on the fiscal stance requires much caution given the large uncertainty about the estimates of potential growth (see below). The increase in total spending is 5.7 per cent in gross terms and 6 per cent in net terms. The impact of the income tax and welfare measures on income distribution is progressive. The range of other tax measures would also seem to have favoured income redistribution overall, even though some tax increases would have regressive impacts.

The restriction in expenditure falls most heavily on capital projects where small declines are forecast, though the level of public investment remains high at

Box 3. Summary of measures contained in Budget 2003

The overall budgetary package of revenues amounted to around € 1.1 billion with expenditures just over € 1.3 billion.

Tax measures

The main provisions included an increase in employee tax credits from € 660 to € 800 and no changes in income tax rates or the standard income tax band. The mortgage interest relief ceiling for first time buyers was increased, as were the age exemption limits. The cost of these measures is estimated to be € 141 million in 2003. The non-indexation of the bands means that this is an effective tax rise when expected wage growth is accounted for. The standard rate of corporation tax was reduced from 16 per cent to 12.5 per cent.

The Pay-Related Social Insurance (PRSI) ceiling was increased from € 38 740 to € 40 420 or around 4.3 per cent, slightly lower than expected wage inflation.

The lower rate of VAT was increased by 1 percentage point to 13.5 per cent, which should yield revenues of about € 187 million in 2003. Excise duties were raised for cigarettes, spirits, alcopops and diesel, and the vehicle registration tax rates were restructured. These changes are estimated to boost revenues by € 311 million in 2003. The combined impact of the increases in the VAT rate and excise duties is expected to add about 0.85 per cent to the consumer price index. There were also a number of changes in the stamp duty rates and thresholds for non-residential property. Stamp duty on cheques and credit, charge and ATM cards was also increased, and a new stamp duty on laser cards was introduced. In total all these stamp duty changes will bring in an additional € 169 million to the Exchequer in 2003. Changes in capital gains payment dates and tax relief will net a further € 270 million in 2003.

Expenditure measures

The expenditure measures announced were considerably less generous than in previous years. Gross spending on public services is estimated to increase by 5.7 per cent, bringing it to just over € 38 billion. Budget day measures accounted for a large proportion of this increase. In particular, social inclusion measures received an extra € 500 million on their pre-Budget estimate. This was mainly due to increases in social welfare, costing € 395 million, and child benefit payments costing € 79 million. The increase in public spending is also due to the € 615 million set-aside for public sector pay under the backdated element of the Benchmarking report. In addition, increased spending on roads of € 209 million was included in the Budget day measures.

about 5 per cent of GNP. The additional revenue sources, derived from increased indirect taxes, under-indexation of the income tax band, changes in the timing of capital taxes and contributions from the Capital Services Redemption Fund, have been mainly used to finance additional current spending rather than capital investment. While the sums allocated to capital investment as a share of output remain substantial by international standards, the more modest growth rates facing the Irish economy over the next few years will require real choices being made between how government expenditure is allocated between consumption and investment purposes.

Apart from the substantial costs of the SSIAs that could increase in the coming years, a significant consideration for the public-finance position through to 2005 will be the impact of the Benchmarking pay proposals for public sector workers (see Box 4).

The Benchmarking exercise has been criticised for having failed to address the recruitment/retention difficulties and equity issues within the public service (Ruane and Lyons, 2002; and O'Leary, 2002). The public sector wage bill already constitutes about half of government net current spending and so it would have a significant impact on the public finances. The cost of the benchmarking pay increases to the end of 2003 was provided for in the 2003 budget with

Box 4. **Benchmarking public sector pay**

Under the terms of the Programme for Prosperity and Fairness, the Public Service Benchmarking Body (PSBB) was established on July 19, 2000. The body was set up to address the perceived problems with the remuneration, recruitment and retention of staff within the public service. The PSBB carried out a detailed examination into the jobs, pay and conditions of public servants and made a comparison with similar jobs in the private sector. The final report, published on June 30, 2002, recommended changes in public service management practices and a range of pay increases.

The recommended pay increases apply to the state's 275 000 public servants. This constitutes almost one-sixth of the Irish workforce. The recommended increases range from 2.5 per cent to as high as 25 per cent for certain public service jobs and averages out at 8.9 per cent. The increases will be phased in between 2003 and 2005. This would represent an increase of just over € 1.1 billion on the public sector pay bill if implemented in full. The body also recommended that 25 per cent of any award be implemented and backdated to the 1st December 2001. The remaining 75 per cent will be conditional on public servants agreeing to recommendations of the Programme of Modernisation and Change. The Programme alters work practices in a number of areas, provides for increased open recruitment to the civil service and requires strong commitment to industrial peace. It also contains verification procedures to ensure the terms are complied with in full. When added to the 7.2 per cent basic increase proposed in the new social partnership agreement, public servants will receive under the terms of the new deal a rise in the range of 9 to 32 per cent with an average of over 16 per cent. Public sector employees, however, face a six-month pay pause in the first half of 2003 and will not receive the final element until mid-2005.

€ 565 million set aside and a further € 50 million provided for other pay and pay-related issues. It is also clear that in the current era of budgetary tightness, any room for manoeuvre in the 2004 budget will be severely restricted due to increases under benchmarking.

The 2003 budget represents a departure from tax-cutting budgets of recent years towards the use of higher taxes to fund expenditure. The budgetary process, however, needs to go further than recognising that current expenditure growth has to be matched by taxation growth. It is imperative that required funding of capital investment growth is put in place to keep it immune from cyclical developments in the public finance position. This requires better control over current expenditure.

Medium-term fiscal position

The deterioration in the public finances from the exceptionally high surpluses of recent years to an anticipated period of deficits is reaffirmed in the Stability Programme Update that accompanied the 2003 budget. The projection for the general government balance is for deficits to rise over the period 2002 to 2005. It remains the case that when measured by the debt to GDP ratio, the Irish debt burden is expected to remain among the lowest within the EU. In contrast to several other EU states, Ireland is not expected to have difficulty in complying with the criteria in the EC Treaty for both fiscal deficit and debt positions over the medium term[12] (see Table 2).

The key strategic objectives of the government are to concentrate resources, within budgetary constraints, on improving the quality of public services and delivering further real improvements to pensioners and people on low incomes; to address the infrastructure deficit in a coherent and structured way; and to sustain the public finances in a healthy state while pursuing a fiscal policy stance that safeguards the competitive position of the economy.

The outlook is for a general government budget deficit of 0.8 per cent of GDP in 2003 followed by deficits of 1.2 per cent of GDP in both 2004 and 2005. The underlying structural budget balance as reported in the Stability Programme Update is expected to improve from a small deficit in 2003 to a small surplus in 2005. This projected budgetary position over the period 2003-05 respects the terms of the Stability and Growth Pact. It reflects an expectation of more limited increases in the overall revenue yield, combined with a desire to sustain infrastructure investment focused on improving the productive capacity of the economy, and otherwise to target expenditure increases at social concerns and at enhancing the quality of key public services. Consistent with the need to maintain a focus on the longer term – and the consequences of ageing societies – the budgetary strategy also envisages that the ratio of debt to GDP will remain below 35 per cent (see Table 3).

Table 2. **Comparison of deficits and debt ratios in the EU**

	Budget balance		National debt	
	2001	2002	2001	2002
Austria	0.2	–0.6	67.3	67.6
Belgium	0.4	0.0	108.5	105.4
Denmark	2.8	1.8	45.4	45.2
Finland	5.1	4.7	43.8	42.7
France	–1.5	–3.2	57.3	59.5
Germany	–2.8	–3.6	59.5	60.8
Greece	–1.4	–1.2	107.0	104.9
Ireland	**1.6**	**–0.1**	**36.7**	**33.5**
Italy	–2.7	–2.5	109.5	106.7
Luxembourg	6.4	2.6	5.6	5.8
Netherlands	0.1	–1.1	52.8	52.5
Portugal	–4.3	–2.7	55.5	58.1
Spain	–0.1	–0.1	56.9	54.0
Sweden	4.6	1.1	54.4	52.4
United Kingdom	0.8	–1.3	38.9	38.4
Euro area	–1.6	–2.3	69.2	69.1
European Union	–1.1	–2.0	63.0	62.5

Note: National debt, Maastricht definition, is gross financial liabilities of the general government. Budget balance is defined as the general government financial balance.
Source: OECD *Economic Outlook* 73 Annex tables.

Table 3. **General government balance and prospective debt ratio**
Per cent of GDP

	2002	2003	2004	2005
General government balance	–0.1	–0.8	–1.2	–1.2
Cyclically adjusted balance[1]	–1.0	–0.4	–0.2	+0.1
Cyclically adjusted balance[2]	–2.2	–1.8	–2.1	–1.8
Debt ratio (year end)	34.1	34.0	34.5	34.9

1. National estimates based on EU agreed methodology.
2. OECD estimates.
Source: Stability Programme Update, December 2002.

The output gap used in the Stability Programme is based on the EU-agreed approach to estimating potential output, which suggests a rather high growth. When the non-cyclical deficit is calculated with the measure of potential growth described in Chapter I, it remains roughly stable. In any case, given the sensitivity of the estimated non-cyclical deficit to the choice of potential growth estimate, which in turn is surrounded with large margins of uncertainty, care should be taken in drawing any conclusions about the fiscal policy stance.

Overall, however, the public-finance position over the next several years looks to be fairly sound. This is partly because the fiscal implications of the ageing of the population are still limited over this period given the favourable demographics delivering low dependency ratios. In addition, the National Pension Reserve Fund (NPRF), which sets aside 1 per cent of GNP annually, had accumulated about 6 per cent of GDP (8 per cent in GNP terms) in assets by the end of 2002. Over the very long term, however, Ireland too cannot escape from the consequences of the population ageing.

The impact of ageing on the public finances

The Irish public finances, in contrast to many other EU states, has the benefit of time on its side as it experiences a "demographic dividend" from a baby boom in the late 1970s. The Long Term Issues Group (LTIG, 1999) considered the impact of ageing on the public finances in light of the demographic trends. The LTIG utilised the 1997 Actuarial Review of Pensions as the source of long-term demographic trends in Ireland as set out in Table 4. The total population is projected to increase up to the year 2026 and to decline relatively slowly thereafter.

Table 4. **Long-term demographic projections for Ireland**

	Total population	Working age group	Old age group	Old age dependency ratio	Overall dependency ratio
	(000's)	(000's)	(000's)	(%)	(%)
1996	3 626	2 013	411	21	80
2006	3 832	2 294	453	20	67
2016	4 012	2 351	584	25	71
2026	4 089	2 331	759	33	75
2036	4 071	2 263	908	40	80
2046	3 949	2 073	1 020	49	90
2056	3 730	1 911	1 018	53	95

Source: LTIG (1999).

Given this demographic profile, the LTIG prepared a "base case scenario" for the period 2000 to 2050 setting out a potential path for the economy and the government budget. In this scenario, an Exchequer surplus would be maintained for about 30 years after which a deficit would emerge – this deficit would rise to 2.3 per cent of GNP by 2050. The debt would be eliminated in about 20 years. It is assumed by the LTIG that in the following years the State will use budget surpluses to increase its cash balances, *i.e.* it will take a "negative debt" position. This negative debt position will peak at 14 per cent of GNP by 2030. Beyond this date, as the Exchequer balance moves into deficit, the negative debt will be unwound and the debt will rise to about 11 per cent of GNP by 2050. The base case scenario indicated that the continuation of a pay-as-you-go approach in state pensions would not place a particularly great burden on the Exchequer within the 50-year horizon considered. At the same time, a scenario of partial funding of pension liabilities showed that public finance positions would be even better than in the base scenario, though the results depended crucially on the assumption that accumulated assets earn a real rate of return 1 per cent above that on national debt. The relatively sanguine nature of these scenarios, however, has to be seen against the large budget surplus that existed when the LTIG work was carried out. Subsequent to the LTIG work, the government decided to set aside 1 per cent of GNP *per annum* in the National Pension Reserve Fund (NPRF).

More recently the EU Economic Policy Committee (EUEPC) in October 2001 outlined projections for public spending on pensions and health/long-term care for all Member States, including Ireland, out to 2050 based on a demographic forecast provided by Eurostat and assumptions on key economic parameters agreed with the Irish government. The EUEPC estimated that demographic changes could increase Irish public spending on pensions from just over 4½ per cent of GNP in 2000 to 9 per cent in 2050 and raise public spending on health and long-term care from just over 6½ per cent of GNP in 2000 to more than 9 per cent in 2050 (Table 5). The increase in pension spending is mainly driven by a rise in the old-age dependency ratio, which nonetheless is projected to remain among the lowest in 2050. A rise in the employment rate and a fall in the benefit ratio (average pension as a ratio of output per worker) are attenuating factors, but their combined impact (1.6 percentage points) is largely offset by an increase in eligibility. Projections for health and long-term care spending are prepared by applying the current pattern of expenditures across age groups to future demographic trends. These projections are hence subject to uncertainties about the future changes in the age-related spending patterns.

Table 5. **Long-term sustainability of public finances**

Per cent of GNP[1]

	2000	2005	2010	2020	2030	2040	2050
Old age pensions	4.6	4.5	5.0	6.7	7.6	8.3	9.0
Health care (inc. care for the elderly)	6.6	7.1	7.2	7.7	8.2	8.7	9.1
				Assumptions			
Labour productivity growth		3.2	2.7	1.8	1.8	1.8	1.8
Real GNP growth		4.7	3.5	2.1	2.2	1.9	1.8
Male 20-64 participation rates	87.9	87.5	87.1	86.3	85.7	84.9	85.6
Female 20-64 participation rates	56.7	56.3	56.4	56.7	61.3	65.6	73.3
Total 20-64 participation rates	72.3	72.0	71.7	71.6	73.6	75.4	79.5
Unemployment rate		5.0	5.0	5.0	5.0	5.0	5.0

1. Pensions/health expenditure expressed as a percentage of GNP.
Source: OECD, Budgetary challenges posed by ageing population 2001.

The estimates concerning pensions have been confirmed in the latest review in June 2002 of the Social Insurance Fund, reflecting the pension and social security contribution system as at end-2000 and assessing prospects over the period to 2056. The report, on a scenario of uprating pensions in line with earnings and before utilising the assets of the NPRF concluded that the existing social security (PRSI) contribution rate (combined employee and employer contributions) would need to be raised by 55.8 per cent (an increase of about 8 percentage points for a standard rate) for the SIF to break even over the full period to 2056. If the whole of the assets of the NPRF is used to meet future social security pensions liabilities from 2026 on, then the required increase in the PRSI rate would be very roughly one-third of this increase (or about 3 percentage points for a standard rate).

The National Strategy Report on the Pension System for Ireland submitted to the European Commission in September 2002 appropriately acknowledged the ageing challenge that Ireland faces, and its implications for financial sustainability. The crucial elements in addressing the "ageing" issue identified included further increases in labour force participation rates – especially among females and older age groups – to sustain employment at its current high level and to continue the policy of five-yearly actuarial reviews of the SIF and NPRF to keep assessment of the extent of the challenge up-to-date.

Control of the public finances and priorities

There are some issues that need to be considered going forward. First, there is a question of whether and how Ireland can maintain its low tax environment. The practice of matching current expenditure growth with revenue growth is going to call for a reassessment of the policy of holding the tax burden at comparatively low levels when there is a need for revenue enhancing measures. Obviously, such measures should ideally be targeted to broaden the tax base, rather than to raise the rates. It remains to be seen how large is the scope for broadening the tax base as it is often politically difficult to bring additional activities into the tax net. Eventually, it will be a matter of deciding how large the role of government should be in providing the services required by its citizens.

Second, the establishment of national priorities also brings with it the responsibility for greater scrutiny and control over public expenditure, particularly in the context of tighter fiscal positions than in recent years. This raises an array of questions concerning the efficiency and effectiveness of the public expenditure management system.

III. Enhancing the effectiveness of public expenditure management

Improving the management of public expenditure has become a key challenge for the Irish government in the context of slower growth in tax revenues and rapidly growing public spending. The deterioration in the public finances from the exceptionally high surpluses of recent years to an anticipated period of deficits, together with rapid increases in current spending in recent years highlight the need to establish a sustainable spending path. Controlling spending will likely remain a difficult task as there is intense public pressure for increased government services such as higher quality health and educational services and better public infrastructure. The demand for such services is unlikely to have adjusted to the slower growth prospects that Ireland faces going forward. As well, wages in the public sector are increasing rapidly under the additional influence of the recently completed public service benchmarking exercise. The need to make large infrastructure investment, in the context of declining EU funding, will also put increased pressure on public finances for some years to come. The wide range of competing demands for expenditures in an environment of slowing revenue growth reinforces the need to clearly establish spending priorities and to ensure that value for money becomes the key criterion in all spending areas. This, in turn, requires further significant improvements to public expenditure management systems, so as to provide the authorities with the tools they need for effective planning and control.

Against this background, this chapter examines the key issues relating to the management of public expenditure in Ireland and discusses an agenda for further reform.[13] The chapter begins with an examination of the trends in public spending and their main determinants, and future challenges. It then discusses the main features of the budget management system and the measures taken recently to correct some of the evident defects in the budget process. This is followed by an assessment of the major efficiency aspects of public spending: human resource management, market-based provision of public services, and the fiscal relations between central and local governments. The subsequent section focuses on the efficiency of spending in two priority areas – health and infrastructure. The chapter concludes by proposing an agenda for future reform.

Figure 8. **General government spending**[1]
Per cent of of GDP

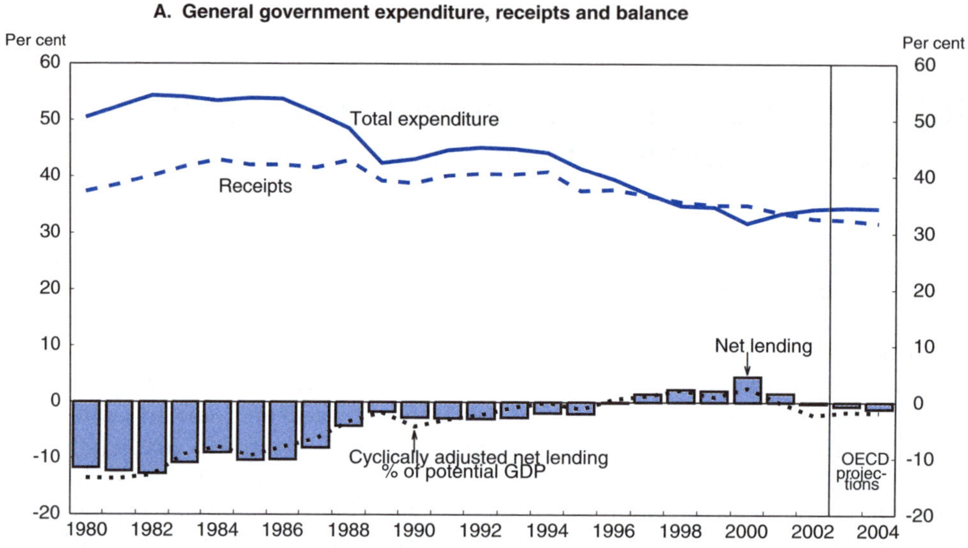

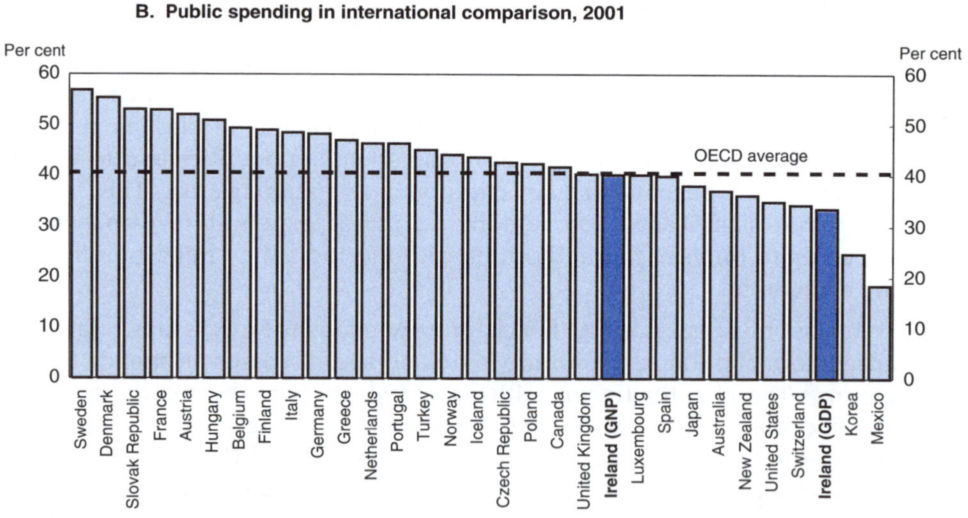

1. Total expenditure is defined as the sum of current outlays and net capital outlays. Data are based on SNA93/ESA95.

Source: OECD.

Trends in public expenditure and forces shaping them

Expenditure trends and international comparisons

After a long period of decline since the early 1980s, the general government spending ratio started to rise from 2000 (Figure 8, Panel A). At 30 per cent of GDP, Ireland's spending ratio was below the OECD average in 2001 (Panel B). But measured against GNP, which is a more sensible base for Ireland in international comparisons,[14] its spending ratio (36 per cent of GNP) was only slightly lower than the OECD average of around 40 per cent of GDP, and about halfway between the United States and the European Union.

The breakdown of government outlays by economic category reveals that there are two main factors that underlie the comparatively low spending level in Ireland (Table 6). *First*, income transfers are low, mainly because of low pension payments, which reflects Ireland's relatively young population (see Table 7).[15] *Second*, relatively low public debt translates into modest interest payments as a share of GNP. Public expenditures on merit goods such as education and health are slightly lower than the OECD average.

The recent increase in public spending reflects rises in both current and capital spending, while interest payments continued to decline (Figure 9). The share of government consumption, albeit still lower than the average of the EU or the OECD as a whole, has been rising due mainly to a steady increase in the public sector wage bill, which constitutes about one-third of government current spending. Increases in both public sector employment and wages contributed to the rise. Between 1997 and 2002, the Exchequer pay bill rose over 70 per cent (Table 8). In particular, there was a sharp increase in the pay bill in the health sector, with a rise of over 100 per cent registered during this period when nominal GNP grew by 82 per cent. The upward trend in investment spending has also accelerated in recent years, reflecting a large increase in the Exchequer funding for infrastructure.

Medium and longer term spending challenges

Upward pressure on public spending is likely to remain strong in Ireland. With increased prosperity, the public demand for improved provision of public services will continue to rise. A key area where pressure will remain strong is health. Despite considerable increase in outputs associated with the enormous increases in government expenditure on the health services in recent years, public dissatisfaction has been expressed concerning long waiting times for access to public hospitals. Public spending will also be under significant pressure to deliver the National Development Plan 2000-2006, which is a major investment programme aimed at alleviating some of the infrastructural constraints on growth with the spending of some € 52 billion (about 70 per cent of GNP in 1999). Under the

Table 6. **General government spending by economic category**
Per cent of GDP in 2001

	Income transfers	Subsidies	Interest payments	Consumption	Net capital outlays	Total outlays
Ireland (GNP)	**10.8**	**1.0**	**1.8**	**16.5**	**6.0**	**36.2**
Ireland (GDP)	9.0	0.8	1.5	13.7	5.0	30.0
Australia	8.9	1.1	2.0	18.5	2.2	32.7
Austria	18.7	2.6	3.9	19.3	5.5	50.0
Belgium (2000)	14.3	1.6	6.5	21.5	2.1	46.0
Canada	11.0	1.5	6.7	18.7	0.2	38.0
Czech Republic	13.2	3.1	1.0	21.0	9.0	47.3
Denmark	17.0	2.0	4.1	25.5	2.1	50.7
Finland	12.5	1.5	2.7	21.0	6.6	44.3
France	17.8	1.2	3.2	23.3	3.3	48.8
Germany	18.9	1.6	3.3	19.0	3.0	45.7
Greece (2000)	16.3	0.2	7.1	15.5	4.9	44.0
Hungary	11.9	5.1	4.9	21.0	6.1	49.1
Iceland	4.2	1.7	3.5	23.3	6.6	39.3
Italy	16.7	1.1	6.4	18.5	3.8	46.4
Japan (2000)	10.0	0.9	3.3	16.7	5.9	36.8
Korea (2000)	3.6	0.3	0.7	10.1	8.3	23.0
Luxembourg	15.1	1.7	0.3	17.5	4.5	39.1
Mexico (2000)	1.7	0.3	3.6	11.1	5.3	21.8
Netherlands	11.6	1.5	3.5	23.2	2.2	42.0
New Zealand (1997)	12.7	0.3	3.1	18.6	3.4	38.2
Norway	13.8	2.2	1.8	20.3	3.2	41.2
Poland (2000)	17.5	0.9	4.0	15.5	4.3	42.3
Portugal	12.5	1.4	3.1	20.7	4.4	42.1
Spain	12.2	1.1	3.1	17.5	3.6	37.5
Sweden	18.1	1.5	3.4	26.7	2.5	52.2
Switzerland (1999)	11.9	1.8	2.1	13.7	4.6	34.1
United Kingdom	13.8	0.5	2.4	19.4	2.3	38.5
United States	11.4	0.5	3.4	15.1	0.9	31.2
Euro area[1]	16.5	1.4	4.1	19.9	3.4	45.3
OECD[1] total	12.8	0.9	3.5	17.3	2.8	37.3

1. Weighted average.
Source: OECD.

Plan, a major investment in social and economic infrastructure is planned, with priorities being given to addressing deficiencies in areas such as housing, roads, water and waste treatment and public transport. But as EU funding is set to decline substantially,[16] sustaining infrastructure investment at a significant level will be challenging, although the increased scope for public private partnerships might ease the pressure to some extent and help boost the efficiency of such outlays.

Over the longer term, spending pressure will also likely accelerate as a result of population ageing and the consequent demands this implies for social

Table 7. Major current government outlays

Per cent of GDP

	Total excluding interest	Merit goods: Total	Merit goods: Education	Merit goods: Health	Merit goods: Other social services	Income transfers: Total	Income transfers: Pensions	Income transfers: Disability and sickness benefits	Income transfers: Family cash benefits	Income transfers: Unemploy-ment	Income transfers: Housing and other benefits
Ireland											
GNP	**33.6**	**10.8**	**4.9**	**5.2**	**0.6**	**12.1**	**4.0**	**1.7**	**1.8**	**3.3**	**1.4**
GDP	29.5	9.5	4.3	4.6	0.5	10.6	3.5	1.5	1.6	2.9	1.2
Australia	30.5	10.9	4.3	5.4	1.2	10.2	4.2	2.1	2.2	1.5	0.2
Austria	46.0	13.8	6.0	5.8	2.0	19.0	12.8	2.5	1.9	1.4	0.4
Belgium	40.4	11.4	5.0	6.1	0.3	18.1	9.8	2.0	2.0	3.8	0.3
Canada	31.0	12.1	5.5	6.6	..	11.2	5.5	1.0	0.8	1.4	2.6
Czech Republic	42.7	11.1	4.1	6.5	0.5	12.7	7.6	2.7	1.6	0.5	0.3
Denmark	47.8	18.8	6.8	6.8	5.2	17.8	6.8	2.6	1.5	5.0	1.8
Finland	44.0	14.0	5.7	5.3	3.0	18.3	8.0	3.5	1.9	3.9	1.0
France	48.4	15.0	5.9	7.3	1.9	19.7	12.2	1.6	1.5	3.1	1.3
Germany	42.7	13.7	4.4	7.8	1.6	18.0	11.0	1.7	1.9	2.6	0.8
Greece	43.3	9.1	3.4	4.7	1.0	16.9	12.2	1.9	1.2	0.7	1.0
Iceland	35.7	16.8	6.5	7.0	3.2	8.2	4.3	1.6	1.2	0.5	0.5
Ireland	29.5	9.5	4.3	4.6	0.5	10.6	3.5	1.5	1.6	2.9	1.2
Italy	39.8	10.8	4.8	5.5	0.5	19.1	15.4	1.7	0.6	1.4	0.0
Japan	32.7	9.8	3.6	5.6	0.6	8.4	6.7	0.6	0.2	0.7	0.2
Korea	22.5	6.7	4.1	2.4	0.3	3.3	2.1	0.4	0.0	0.6	0.2
Luxembourg	39.8	11.3	5.0	5.4	0.9	15.2	8.7	3.1	2.3	0.8	0.3
Netherlands	38.8	12.1	4.5	5.9	1.7	16.1	7.0	3.4	0.8	3.9	1.0
New Zealand	36.1	12.3	6.0	6.1	0.1	13.8	5.4	2.9	2.4	2.2	0.9
Norway	43.9	18.6	6.8	7.1	4.7	15.2	6.3	4.3	2.2	1.4	0.9
Poland	43.4	10.2	5.3	4.6	0.2	18.4	10.2	5.9	0.9	1.0	0.4
Portugal	37.3	11.3	5.6	5.1	0.6	12.5	7.7	2.3	0.6	1.6	0.3
Slovak Republic	50.7	0.5	..	..	0.5	13.3	6.3	3.1	1.8	0.8	1.2
Spain	36.1	10.2	4.4	5.3	0.4	13.9	8.9	2.3	0.3	2.2	0.2
Sweden	49.9	18.6	6.6	6.6	5.4	18.9	8.2	3.5	1.6	3.9	1.7
Switzerland	32.0	13.9	5.4	7.7	0.8	19.9	12.5	3.4	1.2	1.8	0.9
Turkey	36.2	8.2	2.9	5.0	0.2	9.1	6.3	0.3	1.0	1.0	0.5
United Kingdom	34.3	11.6	4.6	5.6	1.3	17.8	10.8	2.8	1.7	0.6	1.8
United States	26.4	11.0	4.8	5.8	0.3	8.2	5.9	1.1	0.2	0.4	0.5
OECD average	38.6	11.9	5.1	5.8	1.4	14.4	8.1	2.4	1.3	1.8	0.8

1. Data is for 1999, or 1998 when not available. Education data always concern 1998. Data is from different sources, so public goods cannot as total government outlays minus merit goods and transfers.
2. OECD estimate based on several sources, so this figure is not entirely reliable.

Source: OECD, Social Expenditure Data base and OECD, *Education at a Glance*, 2001.

Figure 9. **Trends in general government spending**[1]
Per cent of GDP/GNP[2]

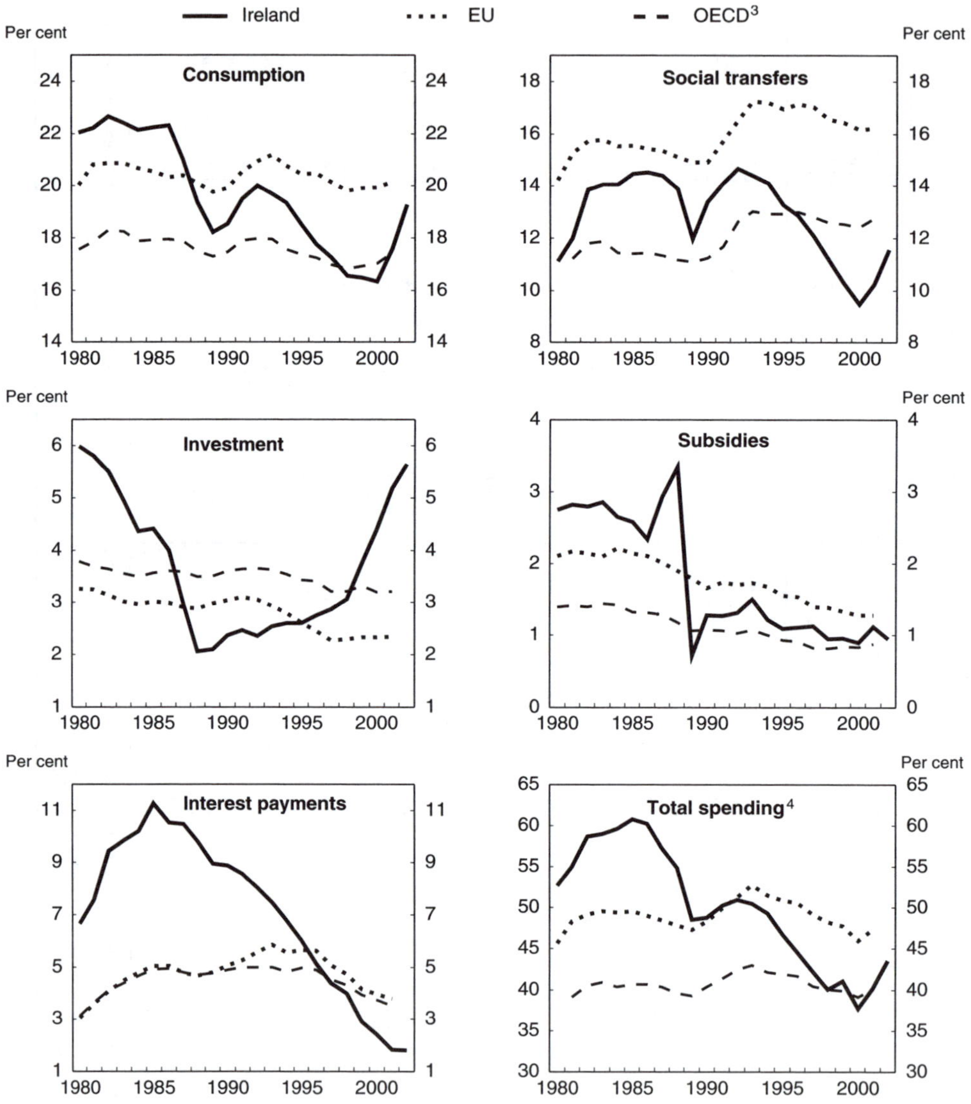

1. Data are based on SNA93/ESA95.
2. GNP is used for the ratios for Ireland.
3. Weighted average (1995 GDP and PPP's) of available countries.
4. Total spending is defined as current outlays plus net capital outlays.

Source: OECD.

Table 8. **Public sector employment and pay**
1997-2002

	1997	1998	1999	2000	2001	2002	% increase 1997-2002
	A. Public sector employment						
Health	65 755	67 895	69 726	75 051	80 879	87 850	33.6
Education	62 100	63 375	64 415	65 937	67 845	71 004	14.3
Civil service	31 030	30 856	31 562	32 733	34 068	36 533	17.7
Security	24 816	24 628	24 541	24 525	24 439	24 258	–2.2
Non-commercial state bodies	8 792	8 815	9 219	9 675	10 442	10 739	22.1
Total Exchequer funded	192 493	195 569	199 463	107 921	217 673	230 384	19.7
% increase over previous year		1.6	2.0	4.2	4.7	5.8	
Local authorities	26 500	26 500	26 900	27 400	28 800	29 300	10.6
Total public service	218 993	222 069	226 363	235 321	246 473	259 684	18.6
% increase over previous year		1.4	1.9	4.0	4.7	5.4	
	B. Sectoral breakdown of Exchequer pay bill Millions of euros						
Health	2 141	2 363	2 703	3 101	3 798	4 306	101.1
Education	1 942	2 053	2 230	2 418	2 831	3 163	62.9
Civil service	920	967	1 009	1 080	1 234	1 388	50.8
Security	793	886	904	966	1 047	1 104	39.3
Non-commercial state bodies	215	237	252	316	401	452	110.7
Total pay	6 010	6 505	7 098	7 882	9 311	10 413	73.2
% increase over previous year		8.2	9.1	11.0	18.1	11.8	

Source: Department of Finance, *Analysis of Exchequer Pay and Pensions Bill 1997-2002.*

spending, notably on pensions, healthcare and associated personal services. Ireland's demographics are more favourable than other European countries, but the longer-term trend towards an ageing population is still an issue. While the elderly dependency ratio is expected to fall further in the near term, it is projected to rise from 20 per cent today, to 25 per cent by 2016 and to 50 per cent by 2050. It is estimated that the Exchequer cost of pensions and healthcare (including care for the elderly) will rise from 11.2 per cent of GNP in 2000 to 14.4 per cent by 2020 and 18.1 per cent by 2050 (see Chapter II). The creation of the National Pensions Reserve Fund will only go part way towards absorbing this extra burden.[17]

Strengthening the budgetary process and control

Controlling aggregate spending

The overriding framework for budgetary policy for Ireland, as for all EU member countries, is the Stability and Growth Pact. This pact commits Ireland to keeping the general government finances close to balance or in surplus and to take corrective action when there is an actual or expected divergence from that objective. Successive governments during the 1990s sought to contain the growth in public spending through the establishment of annual or multi-annual targets.[18] Setting aggregate spending targets, however, has not proved to be very effective in controlling spending in times of revenue buoyancy. A salient feature of the budget outcomes during the 1990s was systematic overshooting in both revenue and spending relative to each year's budget (Figure 10). But spending overruns tended to be more than offset by a larger overshoot in revenue, which made spending control a less compelling issue.[19] However, the situation has changed since 2001, with undershooting revenues highlighting the need to focus on controlling expenditure.

Figure 10. **Overshooting in current revenue and expenditure**
Out-turn less budget estimate as a per cent of budget estimate

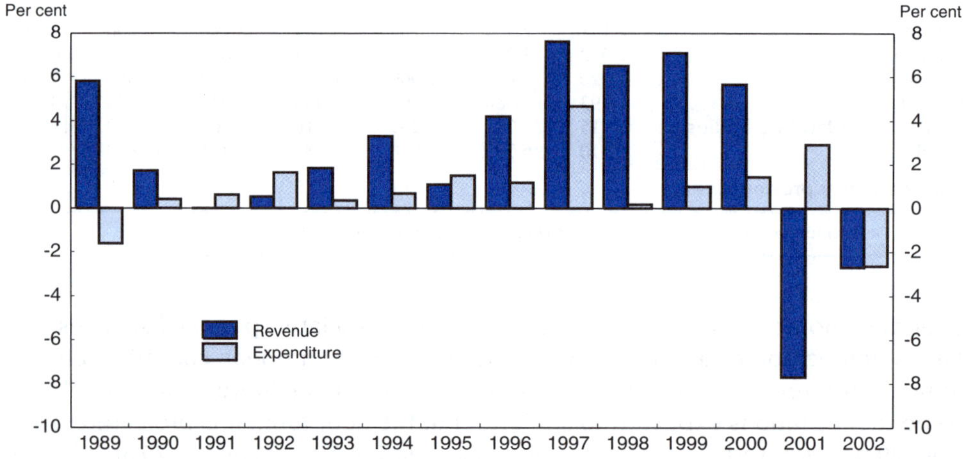

1. Revenue in 1999 excludes 4.7 billion euros from the sale of Telecom Eireann.
Source: Department of Finance.

Facing this changed economic environment, the authorities have made substantial efforts to establish better in-year monitoring and control of expenditure developments, which have contributed to the undershooting of spending in the context of a continued revenue shortfall in 2002. For example, the Minister for Finance provided monthly updates to Government throughout 2002 on emerging spending trends and instructed his officials to maintain contact with departments and to discuss their plans to ensure that spending for 2002 came in on target.

Despite this effort, however, monitoring and controlling of spending have been difficult in some areas, in particular, in the health sector, because of the lack of timely information and because of the demand-led nature of some of the spending.

Aligning policy priorities and budget allocation

At the national level, Ireland has a very elaborate system of establishing and setting priorities in the allocation of resources. This has been conducted for the past 15 years through the media of the National Development Plans and the National Social Partnership Agreements. These Plans and Agreements address the main economic and social priorities confronting the nation at the time and elaborate how available resources are to be allocated to meet these priorities. Each successive government has also published an Agreed Programme for Government that sets out its policy platform for its five-year term. While improvements in the process for priority setting have been made since 2002, there has been a perceived lack of an overall strategic framework at the centre to translate strategic priorities into expenditure allocations at a broad level and to guide individual expenditure decisions in the budgeting process. Further, aligning the policy priorities and actual budget allocation poses a continuing challenge to the Irish budgetary system, which has many of the characteristics of traditional budgetary systems.

Prior to the revisions to the budgeting process in 2002, the priority-setting process for public expenditure was regarded as diffuse and involved very complex negotiations between the Department of Finance and individual spending departments.[20] The budgeting was also characterised as incremental.[21] The reforms to the budgeting process in 2002 involved a move to a more top-down approach to budget formulation in that, for the first time, the Government set expenditure targets for individual spending departments at an early stage in the budget process (see Box 5).

Public expenditure is currently planned within an overall three-year fiscal framework, with projections prepared on a multi-annual basis for both expenditure and revenue. In February 1996, the Government approved the introduction, on a phased basis, of a multi-annual budgetary framework, beginning with Budget 1997. The budget process was revised to begin with the preparation of three-year "No Policy Change" projections of expenditure and revenue,[22] which was subsequently replaced by an "Existing Level of Service" approach in 2002.[23] The current multi-annual budgeting is however characterised by *indicative* multi-annual allocations for planning purposes, and the system of multi-annual financial "envelopes" is not in place.[24] A five-year investment framework is currently being finalised, however, in relation to capital investment spending. The intention is to provide five-year allocation of capital spending on a rolling multi-annual basis starting from the budget for 2004.

Box 5. The budget process in Ireland

The budget formulation process. The fiscal year is from 1 January to 31 December. In April/May of each year, the Department of Finance prepares, in consultation with departments, a multi-annual framework for spending based on the cost of continuing to provide the existing level of services. This feeds into the overall three-year Budgetary Strategy, which is presented by the Minister for Finance to Government in June. In 2002, the Budget Strategy set expenditure targets for each Vote. In July, the Department of Finance requests departments/offices to furnish by the end of that month and detailed estimates for voted current and capital expenditure for the next 3 years. In December, the Minister for Finance announces the Budget which sets out the Government's overall budgetary targets for the following year and outlines revisions to the tax system. The budgetary process continues into the following year. In February of the following year, Revised Estimates are published along with the Public Capital Programme.

The approval process. Parliament does not approve the Budget prior to the start of the fiscal year, a feature common to all Westminster countries. In April of the budget year, Parliament enacts the Finance Bill, which gives legal effect to the tax changes proposed in the budget. In June/July, Parliament votes on detailed Estimates for each service by way of Financial Resolutions. Between June and December, if additional moneys are required by departments, Supplementary Estimates are submitted for approval by Parliament. In December, the Appropriation Bill is passed, which gives statutory effect to the Estimates (including Supplementary Estimates) approved by Parliament. Parliament's authority to amend the government budget is weak, although each department's Estimate must be approved by the legislature. As the spending Estimates are sponsored by Government who has a majority in Parliament, they are generally approved unaltered.

Budget execution and monitoring. The Central Fund Act 1965 authorises the Minister for Finance in every financial year to issue out of the Central Fund and make available sums not exceeding four-fifths of the sums appropriated in the previous year. This facilitates the continuance of operations in anticipation of the relevant vote being passed by Parliament in due course. As soon as an Estimate has been passed by Parliament by means of a Financial Resolution, the full amount of the Estimate may be issued from the Exchequer. It is not necessary to await the enactment of the Appropriation Act. In the course of the budget year, the Department of Finance carries out detailed monthly monitoring of expenditure by spending departments and of trends in the main revenue aggregates. The Minister for Finance submits progress reports to Government on a monthly basis which highlight, where necessary, the need for corrective action to ensure that overall budgetary targets are adhered to.

Audit of government appropriation accounts. The Constitution assigns to the Comptroller and Audit General (C&AG) the responsibility to control on behalf of the State all disbursements and to audit all accounts of moneys administered by or under the authority of Parliament. The C&AG is required to audit the Appropriation Accounts of Government Departments and present copies of the audited Appropriation Accounts to Parliament not later than 30 September in the year following the financial year to which they relate. The Public Accounts Committee (PAC), a select committee of Parliament, examines the C&AG's reports and presents a report to Parliament. A formal reply to a report of the PAC is prepared by the Department of Finance in consultation with the department(s) concerned. The PAC's recommendations carry much weight, although Government is not in the last resort obliged to accept them.

The authorities have made attempts to introduce public expenditure reviews to facilitate strategic prioritisation. In 1997 the Government decided to review all public expenditure over a three-year period under the Expenditure Review Initiative (ERI). The idea was that this review would provide a systematic analysis of what was actually being achieved by each spending programme from a results perspective, which could become a basis on which more informed decisions could be made on the allocation of resources within and between programmes. The first phase of the ERI was carried out over 1997-2001. Over 70 reviews were completed covering about one quarter of Government's discretionary spending. However, the results seem to have been less than satisfactory. The Comptroller and Auditor General's report (2001), which provided a value-for-money review of the ERI, found that there was very little evidence of change in expenditure patterns as a result of the reviews and indeed very few reports proposed substantial revision of priorities. This result might not be surprising given that departments are likely to have very limited incentives to report areas of low priorities, which might mean a cut in budget allocation for those programmes. The experience of other OECD countries also suggests the difficulty of achieving real changes when expenditure reviews are done by departments themselves without being given more explicit targets set by the centre.[25]

Further efforts have been made to strengthen the role of expenditure reviews, following a review of the process by the Department of Finance, which included consideration of the value for money study by the Comptroller and Auditor General. In 2001, the Government approved revised arrangements for the next phase of the ERI, which involved laying down criteria for the selection of programmes for review, the provision of central supports in terms of training and networking, arrangements for quality control and the undertaking of cross-departmental reviews. In May 2002, the Government approved the expenditure review topics proposed for the first year of the next three-year planning horizon (2002-2004). In selecting topics for review, the emphasis was on programmes that involved significant levels of expenditure and programmes where the external environment had changed substantially since they were introduced. In addition, in 2002, the Government took a further initiative by appointing an independent Estimates Review Committee – comprising three former senior civil servants – to make an overall assessment of spending proposals from all departments and offices, from a "whole of government" perspective.[26]

Reforming management practices in the public service

Ireland has been implementing a wide-ranging public service modernisation programme under the Strategic Management Initiative (SMI) launched in 1994. The implementation framework for the SMI was established in "Delivering Better Government (DBG)" published by the Co-ordinating Group of Secretaries, established under the SMI, in 1996. The objective of the changes proposed is "to create a performance-oriented Civil Service that responds effectively to the needs of the Government and clients at all levels and is characterised by flexible working arrangements and practices." SMI is regarded as the most successful reform of the Irish Public Service since the foundation of the independent state (OECD, 2001c). But progress has been uneven, and an evaluation of the SMI finds that it has been more successful with outward-oriented issues (*i.e.* openness, transparency and accountability; quality customer service; and regulatory reform) but less successful with internal systems reform (*i.e.* human resource management, financial management and information systems management).[27] In response to the recommendations contained in the report on the evaluation of the SMI, the Government decided to give the SMI Implementation Group of Secretaries General the task of developing a new vision statement, strategy and action plan for the civil service up to 2007. This next phase of the modernisation programme is to build on initiatives that are already under way and to focus on achieving accelerated progress in implementing the reforms related to internal systems management. The parties to the new social partnership agreement *Sustaining Progress* have committed themselves to co-operate with this new phase of modernisation in the civil service.

The central thrust of the SMI is a shift in focus from inputs to outputs and outcomes in public management. Government departments and offices have been encouraged to adopt modern management practices that entail making explicit strategic statements about function and policy goals and translating them into business plans. The Public Service Management Act, enacted in 1997, was aimed at making the public service system transparent and more effective by clarifying the allocation of authority, accountability and responsibility within the system. The Act specifies that responsibility for planning outcomes and outputs lies with the Minister, while the Secretary General will be responsible for managing the Department, *i.e.* producing outputs as determined with the Minister.[28] Promoting user-orientation of the public service has also been a major objective. Quality customer service has been encouraged through the articulation of customer service principles and the publication of Customer Action Plans. The transparency and accountability of the public service has also been greatly enhanced with the enactment of the Freedom of Information Act in 1997 and the Committees of the Houses of the Oireachtas (Compellability, Privileges and Immunities of Witnesses) Act, 1997.

Progress has been, however, relatively slow with respect to devolution of authority and accountability within the civil service. Although the SMI/DBG envisaged a large degree of financial devolution to line departments/offices in the context of a multi-annual financial envelope system, this system is yet to be implemented, as discussed above. The ability to carry forward savings from one fiscal year to the next remains limited as recouping savings is possible only in administrative spending.[29] In the Budget 2003, however, the Minster for Finance stated that where Departments secure savings as a result of specific efficiency measures or steps they have taken to curtail a programme, these savings should, as a general rule, be available for other high priority programmes within the same Department.

The steps to introduce managerial flexibility and performance orientation make it important to strengthen accountability for results. However, the input-based budget classification system, combined with the lack of performance indicators, makes the evaluation of performance difficult. Furthermore, the absence of adequate, comparable information systems in the public service hinders ongoing monitoring and assessment of the efficiency and effectiveness of how services are provided. The ability to undertake value for money examinations of public expenditure on a regular basis is also frequently constrained by the absence of performance information in a usable format. Addressing these issues, a new Management Information Framework (MIF) is being developed and is due to be in place by 2005. The development of the new MIF is a significant initiative that seeks to address the problem of a lack of performance information by equipping Departments with a system of financial accounts, integrated with a system of output measurement.[30] Meanwhile, the institutional framework for ensuring accountability for performance has been improved. The Comptroller and Auditor General (Amendment) Act 1993 empowered the Comptroller and Auditor General to carry out value for money audits on Government Departments and other public bodies. The value for money audits, which are submitted to the Public Accounts Committee of Parliament, focus on the economy and efficiency of operations and the adequacy of management systems to appraise the effectiveness of operations.

Improving the cost effectiveness of public spending

Reforming human resource management

The SMI/DBG in 1996 set out a radical blueprint for transforming the human resource management function in the civil service. The central components of the programme included: greater autonomy and responsibility to line departments for human resource matters; a new performance management system to support the delivery of quality services to the public; new arrangements for recruitment and promotion; flexibility in atypical recruitment; and increased emphasis on staff training and development. While the programme envisaged radical reforms to bring modernisation and flexibility to the civil service, overall the pace of change has been remarkably slow.[31] The public sector labour market is still characterised by a lack of flexibility. There is limited linkage between performance and reward/recognition, as senior managers do not yet have the tools to reward excellence or tackle under-performance.[32] One limitation has been the terms and conditions of employment under the Civil Service Regulation Act, 1956, which reinforce a presumption of permanent tenure of civil servants. It thus makes it difficult to dismiss or discipline staff who consistently under-perform.

The public sector benchmarking exercise and the subsequent pay increases for public sector employees (see Chapter II) raise concerns about the means to link pay increases with corresponding increases in performance and productivity of the public service. It has been agreed that the payment of the final two phases of the pay increases recommended by the Public Service Benchmarking Body (plus the general round increases under the new agreement) will be dependent on verification of satisfactory implementation of the agenda for modernisation set out in the new social partnership agreement, which has proposed a new ambitious package of reform (see Box 6). Given the limited progress made in this area in the past, it will be particularly important to develop the link between public sector pay increases and the modernisation of the public service.

Introducing competition and market signals in publicly funded services

Many OECD countries have introduced market-based principles into the public sector with the aim of enhancing efficiency in publicly funded services through competition (Lundsgaard, 2002). Ireland has followed this trend in recent years, but there is still much room for further exploiting the benefits of market mechanisms.

The use of contracting out has been limited

Contracting certain existing activities to private operators or carrying out public activities on a commercial footing can promote efficiency and generate cost savings. Contracting out for the provision of publicly funded services and support functions (*e.g.* building maintenance and street cleaning) has not been systematically used in Ireland. Nonetheless, there have been more cases of contracting out of non-core functions in recent years. For example, in the area of public transport, vehicle testing has been contracted out to a private company since January 2000.[33] In addition, the management of parking, clamping, etc. in Dublin has been contracted out to a private company, which has significantly reduced the amount of illegal on-street parking and raised additional revenue for the City Council.[34] In many local authority areas, waste collection has been contracted out to private agents. In addition, contracting out in infrastructure development and operation is being pursued under the Public Private Partnerships (PPP), which is discussed in the section below.

User charges can be extended to other services

Traditionally, concerns about income distribution or exclusion of some groups from public services have limited the scope for user charging in Ireland. But

Box 6. The new partnership agreement related to human resource management in the civil service

The new social partnership agreement *Sustaining Progress* 2003-2005 covers a number of areas related to the human resource management practices in the civil service. Some of the important agreements include the following:

Modernisation of human resource management practices. The agreement envisages that legislation will be introduced by December 2003 to bring new management practices into effect by updating the Civil Service Regulation Act, 1956. These reforms will enable the Secretary General of a Department to perform all functions pertaining to appointments, performance, discipline, and dismissal of civil servants below Principal Officer level and provide that staff, at and above Principal Officer level (other than those appointed by Government) may be dismissed by the Minister only on the recommendation of the Secretary General. In the context of this new legislation, the parties agree to extend the scope of the Unfair Dismissals Acts to cover civil servants, to widen the range of disciplinary sanctions, and to have a fuller range of sanctions available in serious cases of underperformance.

Addressing skills shortages and strengthening recruitment practices. Open recruitment will be introduced for appointments above existing entry levels. One-year contacts will be extended to all new recruits to the civil service starting on 1 January 2004. In addition, a number of specific measures have been agreed to address the problem of short supply in specific areas such as IT and financial management.

Improvements in promotion systems. It is agreed that discussions will take place so that greater use of competitive, merit-based promotions within Departments will be introduced and developed over the life of the Agreement in order to provide wider career development opportunities for civil servants. Other agreements include a reduction of the existing service requirements in respect of eligibility for promotion by one year subject to a minimum of two years service; and an increase in the proportion of posts filled under mobility provisions of interdepartmental promotion competitions from 33.3 per cent to 40 per cent.

experience in other OECD countries show that user charges can be an effective means to reduce excessive demand for some publicly funded services by making households more cost conscious, while avoiding poverty traps. Ireland has been employing new or increased user charges in recent years to improve efficiency and control costs. For example, all local authorities now charge a levy for waste collection. However, except for a few cities, the charges are currently levied on a flat-rate basis rather than on a pay-per-bag basis, providing households little incentive to reduce waste production (see Chapter IV). The government's plan to introduce weight/volume-based waste charging throughout the country should help promote waste reduction. In the health sector, a range of charges have been increased, including bed charges, accident and emergency charges and medicine charges.[35]

Despite the recent move, the State continues to provide a wide range of services either free or at low cost and, in some cases, it would be appropriate to increase charges or introduce new charges. Water charges are a case in point. Ireland is unique among OECD countries in not charging domestic consumers for water services.[36] Meanwhile, drinking water quality and sewerage treatment requirements are becoming more stringent and water/sanitary services are becoming more expensive to provide and operate. A charging regime in this area could contribute to a more efficient use of what is becoming an increasingly expensive resource. Moreover, the long-term objective in relation to water and sewerage services should be to encourage more sustainable patterns of consumption.

The public education system heavily subsidises tertiary education in Ireland. Third-level fees were abolished in 1995 to increase access to tertiary education for disadvantaged groups. While in many OECD countries there has been a trend of an increasing proportion of costs of tertiary education borne by participants, Ireland is exceptional in having eliminated fees for undergraduate students. However, studies in Ireland suggest that this policy is yet to show noticeable results in terms of broadening inclusion from all sectors of the society. The rates of admission to higher education still vary significantly by family socio-economic backgrounds, and students from well-off areas and fee-paying schools dominate the larger universities.[37] This has raised a considerable debate as to the no-fee policy on equity grounds.[38] Such heavy subsidisation is questionable on both equity and efficiency grounds, in particular, given that the private return to education is much higher than the social rate of return for those who have a university degree (Blöndal *et al.*, 2002). The question of re-introducing third-level fees for those full-time students whose families can afford to pay is under consideration by the Department of Education and Science. It was also announced in 2002 that the student registration charge would rise by almost 70 per cent.[39] At the same time, the government might consider introducing government-backed student loans. The introduction of loan-based systems has been shown to be successful in generating income and in increasing access in a number of OECD countries.[40]

A wider use of benchmarking and other market instruments could be beneficial

The use of other market-type instruments such as benchmarking and other choice schemes within the public sector is generally limited in Ireland. Benchmarking of government agencies, which tend to be exempt from the pressures to perform more efficiently and effectively, can be an effective means to exert such pressures in a constructive way. In recent years benchmarking techniques have been increasingly used to provide performance indicators for local authorities. A wider use of benchmarking would also be beneficial in the key spending areas such as health and education (see Box 7). For example, benchmarking could be employed to assess and improve the performance of tertiary education institutions in Ireland.

Box 7. Mechanisms to introduce competitive pressures on providers of publicly funded services

OECD countries have used a range of market-type instruments to introduce competitive pressures on providers of publicly funded services, with the aim of better responding to the users' needs and improving cost efficiency. The arrangements applied vary across OECD countries and also tend to differ according to the type of service areas. This box provides some examples of these alternative arrangements for provision of publicly funded services.

Benchmarking. Benchmarking refers to the technique of comparing performance levels across providers of similar services to identify best practices. By allowing comparisons to be made across providers of similar services, benchmarking can be an effective means to exert competitive pressures, in particular if funding is aligned with performance. This instrument could be particularly useful in core collective services, such as defence, police and core public administrative functions where governments often have to rely on monopoly provision through an incumbent public agency. In the health and education sectors, a number of countries have recently developed quality and cost indicator systems for benchmarking. In some decentralised countries such as Norway and Sweden, efforts have been made to provide local citizens information on the coverage and costs of public services across municipalities, allowing them to put pressures on their administration to improve the cost-effectiveness of their spending programme.

Contracting out and competitive tendering. The appropriate use of contracting out and competitive tendering can raise efficiency and thereby result in substantial cost savings by exerting competitive pressures on service providers. These savings arise in part from efficiency gains from economies of scale and specialisation which can be exploited through outsourcing whereas tendering introduces more competition. In order for the gains to be made, however, the contracts should be carefully designed and the benefits from efficiency gains should be weighed carefully against transaction costs which are likely to be high when outputs are difficult to define and assess. The services best suited to contracting out are those with clearly definable outputs, such as waste collection, road maintenance, street cleaning, wage administration, computer services, maintenance of buildings and equipment, and operation of urban transport systems. A number of empirical studies have documented that contracting out and competitive tendering can allow a constant quality of service to be provided at lower costs, especially for technical services like waste collection and cleaning (Lundsgaard, 2002).

Introducing user choice (including voucher schemes). Allowing users individually to choose among alternative suppliers, while maintaining public funding, is another way of spurring competition among providers. The areas where this instrument has often been introduced include: pre-school nursery education, education and training, health care, social housing, and social/long-term care (Cave, 2001). For example, users can be given a voucher allowing them to spend it only for a particular service, but with a wide range of alternative suppliers (*e.g.* medical practices or schools). In practice, explicit voucher schemes with physical coupons are very rare, but OECD countries use a set of arrangements that allow

Box 7. **Mechanisms to introduce competitive pressures on providers of publicly funded services** (*cont.*)

users to choose among different suppliers of publicly funded services. The examples of these implicit voucher systems include: school choice programmes whereby funding for a school is based on the number of users, fee-for-services for health care suppliers reimbursed by the social security system, per-user subsidies for private nursing homes, income-dependent benefits earmarked for the purchase of child care in approved centres and tax credits for documented private schools fees. However, the degree to which user choice creates competitive pressures on suppliers depends much on whether public funding per user is levelled across public and private suppliers, which may often not be the case.

Improving the effectiveness of spending by sub-national government

The Irish public administration is one of the most centralised among OECD countries, with local government subject to more strict statutory, administrative and financial control than its counterparts elsewhere. There are 34 county/city local authorities that are the main providers of local government services. In addition, 80 town authorities carry out a representative role for the town with a varying range of local government functions.[41] These authorities in Ireland have one of the largest population sizes per basic unit among EU countries, but carry-out a narrower range of functions than elsewhere.[42] Local authorities are mainly responsible for the provision of infrastructure and services including roads, social housing, water supply and sewerage, planning and environmental protection.[43] They are not primarily responsible for such functions as education, health, police and social welfare, which are the responsibility either of central government departments or of separate local or regional bodies.[44] Local authorities are subject to tight financial control by the central government through the balanced budget rule for current expenditure and the requirement that local borrowing be subject to the approval by the central government.

Local authority funding system could be improved to promote allocative and cost efficiency

The abolition of the local property tax on domestic dwellings in 1977 and on agricultural land in 1983 led to a highly centralised system of financing of local authorities in Ireland (see Box 8). The share of tax revenue in local government finance in Ireland is one of the lowest among OECD countries, while the share of central government grants is among the highest (Figure 11). Although local authorities

Box 8. Local authority funding

In the 1970s, property taxes were charged on commercial, domestic and agricultural property and these, combined with fees and charges, provided 50 per cent of local authority needs from local sources. Legislation enacted in 1978 abolished the local property tax on domestic dwellings and replaced it by a central government grant – the Rate Support Grant. With effect from 1983, the property tax on agricultural land was terminated as a result of a court judgement. Since then, the levying of local property tax has been confined to commercial and industrial property.

Prior to 1988, local authorities borrowed (mainly from state agencies) for various capital purposes such as housing, water and sewerage, libraries, etc., with state subsidy to assist them in paying the resulting loan charges. In 1988 this system was replaced by direct capital grants from the central government for the relevant projects. There are four main sources of local authorities' current income:

Tax revenues. Proceeds from commercial rates, which are levied annually by local councils on the value of commercial premises, are the only source of local tax revenues. In general, local authorities are free to decide on the overall level of rates collected by them annually. Between 1999 and 2002, caps had been set by the central government on the overall maximum level of rate increases that can be applied by a local authority. But starting from 2003, no such cap is set by the central government.

Non-tax revenues. Non-tax revenue receipts of local authorities come from the provision of a wide variety of goods and services of which the most significant are rents and part of the proceeds of sales of local authority housing, repayments by borrowers of house purchases and improvement loans and charges for water supplies, refuse collection and sewerage facilities. Non-tax revenues comprise about 30 per cent of local authority revenues. Local authorities are generally free to determine the charges payable for miscellaneous receipts, except for domestic water charges which were abolished nationally in 1997. The responsibility for paying domestic water and sewerage charges was transferred from domestic water users to the central government with effect from 1 January 1997.

Earmarked grants. Earmarked grants cover all of local authorities' capital expenditure and a substantial portion of current expenditure. Most earmarked grants cover 100 per cent of actual expenses, although for smaller grant schemes, local authorities may be asked to co-finance – typically 25 per cent – according to the matching rate set by the central government. The bulk of earmarked grants go to local capital projects, *e.g.* roads and public housing.

Block grants. A system of block grants was modified in 1997, with the introduction of the local Government (Equalisation) Fund which was subsequently amended in 1999 and became the Local Government Fund. The Local Government Fund provides finance to local authorities as general-purpose grants and for non-national roads and is itself financed from two sources: an Exchequer contribution and the full proceeds of motor taxation. The general-purpose allocations from the Local Government Fund are determined in part by a "needs and resources" model. The model decides allocations based on each local authority's needs (set against expenditure targets at service level) and resources (set against the capacity to raise resources through other means). This is effected by analysing each authority's current expenditure and income patterns (including income from commercial rates) for each service and adjusting each authority's actual expenditure and income towards the standard for that service. The difference between expenditure and income for each authority identified by this process indicates the funding that should be provided through general-purpose allocations. This model is gradually being refined to customise it to expenditure and income conditions in each local authority.

Figure 11. **Composition of subnational government financial resources**
As a percentage of total financial resources, 1999[1]

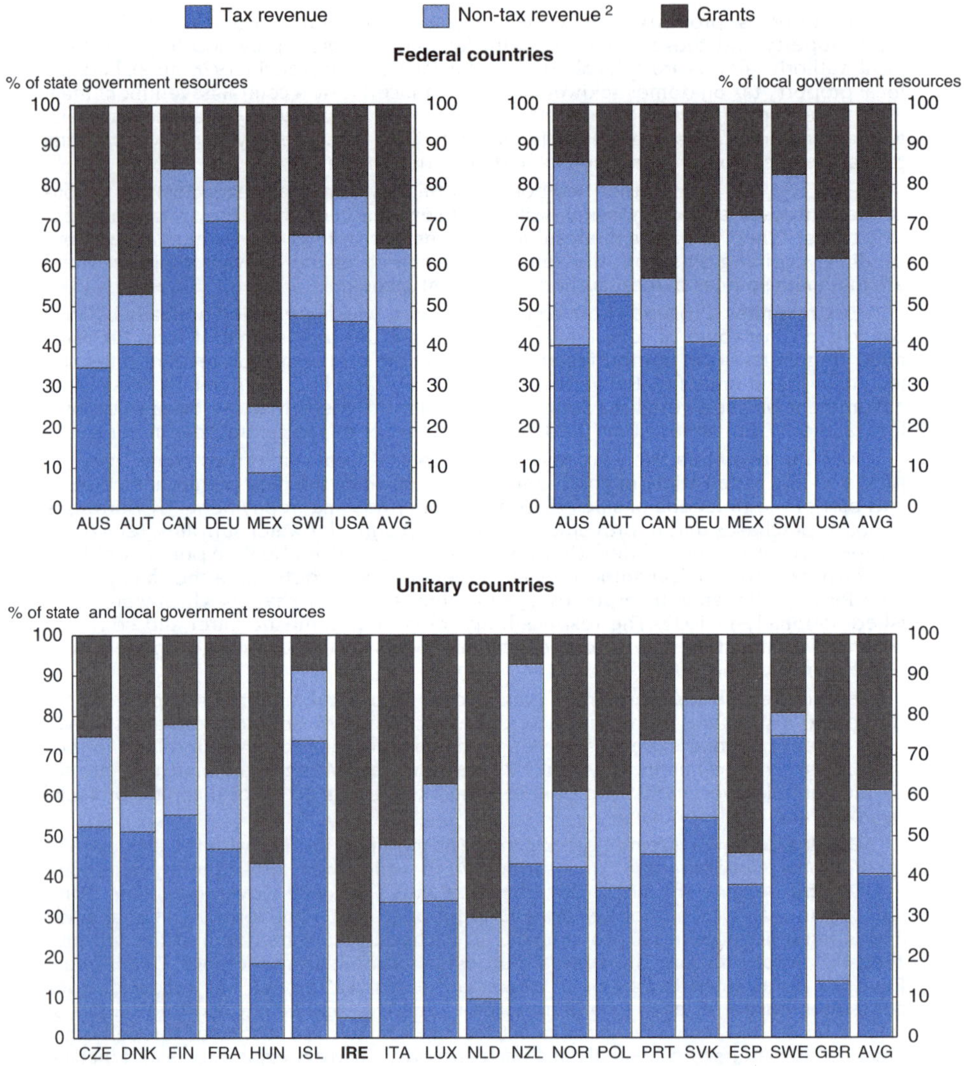

1. For non-tax revenue: 1984 for Switzerland, 1997 for France, Ireland, Luxembourg, Netherlands and Spain, 1998 for Iceland, Norway, Portugal and United Kingdom.
2. Non-tax revenues include: operating surpluses of public entreprises controlled by sub-national governments; property income; fee, sales and fines; contributions to government employee pension funds and capital revenues.

Source: OECD Revenue Statistics, 1965-2001.

have been increasingly financed by local non-tax revenues, the current financing system allows very limited discretion to local authorities to determine local service and related expenditure levels.

The absence of a local property tax on households could potentially have negative implications for local government accountability as local households do not directly pay for a significant portion of the services provided by local authorities. Together with the absence of domestic water and sewerage charges, this could also put excessive upward pressure on the demand for local services.[45] The large reliance of local authorities on central government grants may also have negative implications for allocative and cost efficiency. A large proportion of these central government grants is funded as earmarked grants, *i.e.* tied to specific expenditure programmes. Earmarked grants are particularly important for counties which collect a relatively low amount of commercial rates due to the abolition of rates on agricultural lands in the 1980s (Figure 12). While the use of earmarked grants may serve to internalise externalities associated with infrastructure provision, heavy reliance on them may contribute to inefficient local spending. In particular, the fact that most of the grants cover 100 per cent of *ex post* actual expenses may weaken incentives to contain costs. The prevalence of earmarked grants also permits little flexibility needed to enhance allocative efficiency as funds cannot be shifted to other uses in accordance with changing priorities.

The newly established funding system, called the Local Government Fund, represents a significant move to introduce equalisation between local authorities through formula-based block grants. It has also injected a measure of stability and certainty into local government financing.[46] The allocation formula will continue to need refinement so that the formula sets the standards, where possible, for different services while allowing authorities to make decisions based on local preference.

Local government reforms have been underway

A number of measures have been introduced to strengthen the accountability framework for the performance of local authorities in recent years, which have significantly enhanced the quality of performance management systems at the local level.[47] *First*, regular value-for-money audits, conducted by the Value for Money (VFM) Unit in the Department of the Environment and Local Government, have been a feature of local government management in recent years.[48] *Second*, significant investment has been made in the development of new financial management and costing systems. Accounting procedures are being switched from a cash to an accrual basis. A new costing system that generates information on the true cost of providing individual services will commence development in 2003 and will be rolled out to local authorities as soon as possible thereafter. *Third*, a greater emphasis is being placed on performance management at local government level.

Figure 12. **Local authorities' current revenue by source**

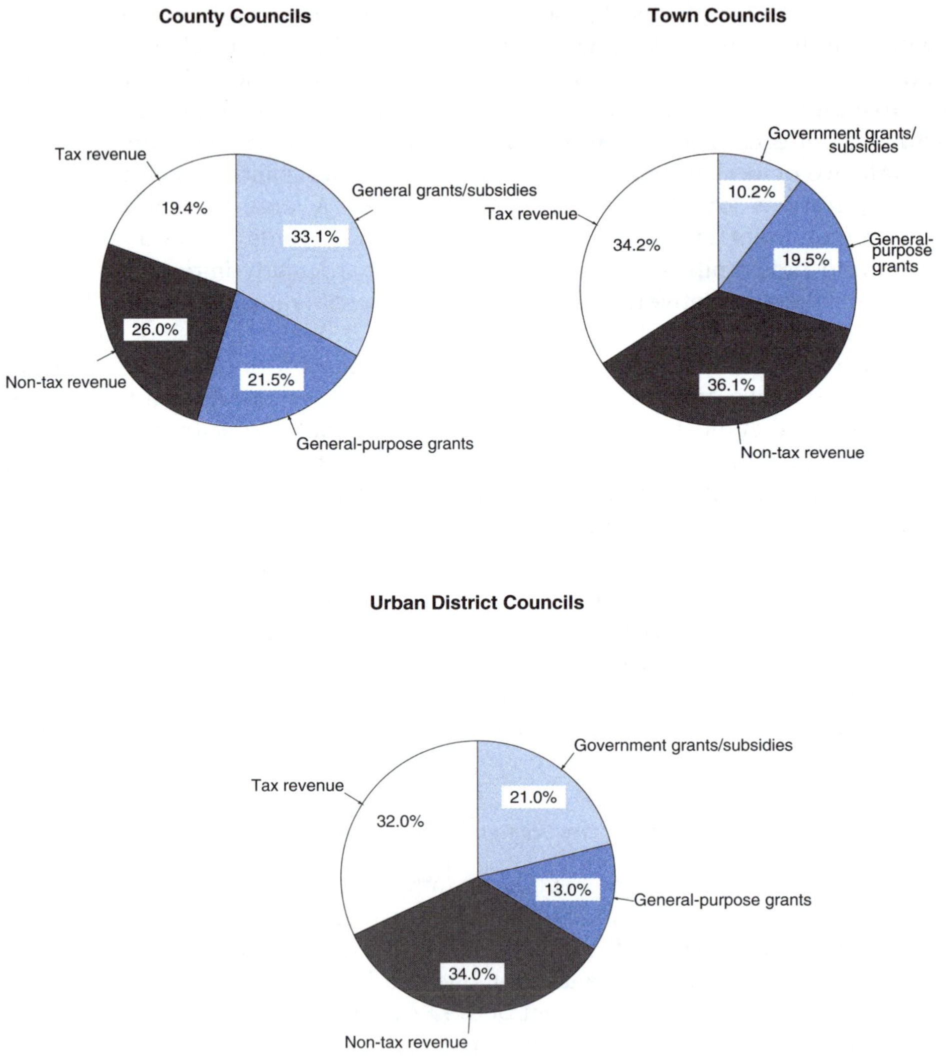

1. Government grants/subsidies are a mixture of earmarked and block grants. While detailed breakdowns are not available, most of them are estimated to be earmarked grants.

Source: Department of Environment and Local Government, *Local Authority Estimates 2002.*

Local authorities are now required to publish their performance results in their annual reports.

Co-ordination and co-operation of sub-national public bodies could be improved

A salient feature of the structure of sub-national public sector in Ireland is the proliferation of semi-autonomous public bodies that operate separately from local authorities at either local or regional level.[49] Many of the business and commercial development functions are performed by these public bodies such as the Fishery Boards, tourism and industrial development agencies. Most of these bodies have been set up in an *ad hoc* manner and, until now, have rarely been merged or eliminated. Concerns have often been raised about the absence of a clear overall framework, which tends to create overlapping functions or gaps in coverage giving rise to duplication of services and some confusion for potential clients.[50] This suggests considerable scope for streamlining the public bodies or transferring some of their roles to local government upon a thorough review. It will be also important to make clear their roles and functions to enhance the effectiveness of the co-ordination and co-operation between national/local authorities and other public bodies.

There is also scope for increasing co-operation between local authorities. The major services provided by local authorities in Ireland such as roads, waste management and planning have implications beyond the boundaries of individual local authorities. Horizontal co-operative arrangements for joint provision of public services could be one way to internalise spillover effects in these service areas. While some co-operation already exists[51], there is considerable scope for enhancing level of co-operation and co-ordination among local authorities, in particular, at the regional level. The question of the establishment of a new regional body to co-ordinate land use and transport in the Dublin area is currently being considered by the government. Continued efforts in this direction will be necessary, but the role and responsibility of this body should be clearly defined and continuously monitored. Efforts have also been made to develop a shared strategy of development by establishing Country/City Development Boards with wide representation. A key role of the Boards is the co-ordination of public and local development services at county/city level.

Concerns have also been raised about the inefficiencies arising from the fragmented structure of local authorities in areas such as maintenance of social housing, road repair, water supply and sewage (OECD, 2001a). Until now, local authorities have rarely been merged or restructured,[52] but there has been some shift of functions from sub-county to county level. For example, with effect from 1 January 2004 water services functions are to be consolidated at country/city level, which is considered to be the lowest practical level of efficient service provision. Further efforts in this direction will be needed to enhance the efficiency of local spending, but serious consideration should also be given to merging the smaller local authorities as a way to internalise spillovers of local services.

Challenges of improving spending outcomes in healthcare and infrastructure

Controlling spending and improving efficiency in healthcare

Controlling spending while improving efficiency in healthcare has become one of the most pressing issues in Ireland, and a number of wide-ranging studies on both organisational structures and financial management in the Irish health service are under way. Health expenditure has increased on a significant scale throughout the 1990s, registering one of the most rapid spending increases among OECD countries despite a younger age structure (Figure 13). It is estimated that per capita spending had caught up with the EU average by 2001. The rise in current public health expenditure was particularly sharp for the last five years, with an increase of 70 per cent in real terms, which resulted in substantial improvements in health outputs. For example, between 1997 and 2002, day patient activity increased by 65 per cent and the number of in-patient beds and in-patient discharges rose by 3 per cent and 4 per cent, respectively.[53] The Irish population is in relatively good health, rating close to or above OECD averages in some selected indicators on health care outcomes and resources as shown in Table 9. Acute-care beds per 1 000 population are lower in Ireland than the OECD average, but the average length of stay is shorter in Ireland. Despite the large increase in spending and associated increases in the quality and availability of health services, public perception remains critical, focusing in particular on long waiting lists for access to public hospitals and delays in accident and emergency departments. The general perception is that the spending increase has, at best, only resulted in a modest improvement in services.

A lack of comprehensive information and transparency remains a major weakness

One of the major weaknesses of the health system is the lack of comprehensive information about the distribution of resources and performance in this system, which seems to have contributed to the public perception about inefficiencies. In particular, the public dissatisfaction with long waiting times for access to public hospitals seems to have been exacerbated by a prevailing perception that the access to, and quality of, care for public patients in public hospitals has been hindered by the encroachment of private patients on public beds. Indeed the available evidence indicates that more private patients are accessing public facilities beyond the proportion of hospital beds designated for use by private patients (see Box 9). It will be important to enforce the regulations which limit the share of public beds occupied by private patients to safeguard the access to care for public patients in public hospitals and to improve the satisfaction with the

Figure 13. **Trends in health care expenditure**

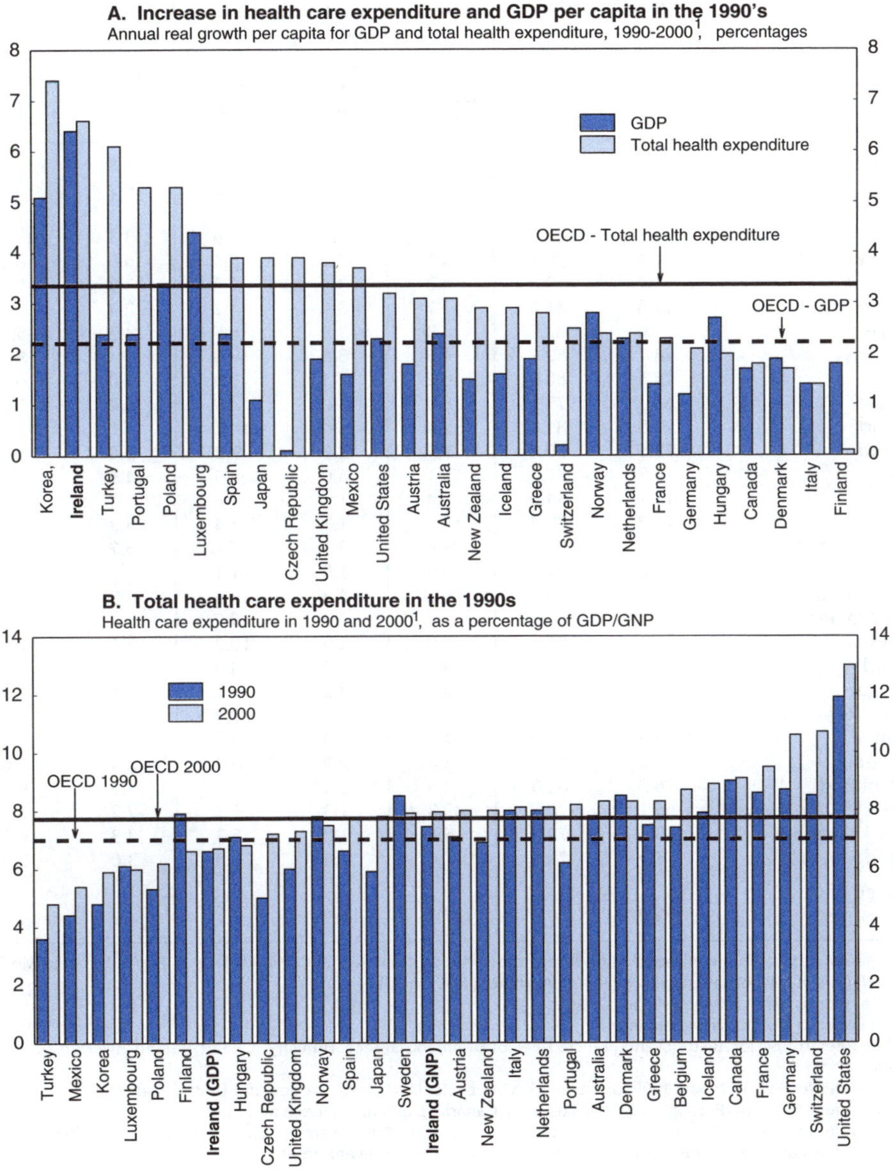

1. 1990-98 for Sweden and Turkey, 1990-99 for Luxembourg and Poland, 1991 to 2000 for Hungary. 1992-2000 for Germany.

Source: OECD Health Data 2002.

Table 9. Selected health care outcomes, resources and utilisation[1]

	Life expectancy		Infant mortality	Medical personnel (per 1 000 population)		Acute-care hospitals	
	Males 1999[2]	Females 1999[2]	Deaths per 1 000 live births 1999[3]	Practising physicians 2000[4]	Practicing nurses 2000[5]	Beds per 1 000 population 2000[6]	Average length of stay 2000[7]
Australia	76.2	81.8	5.7	2.5		3.8	6.2
Austria	75.1	80.9	4.4	3.1	9.2	6.2	6.3
Belgium	74.4	80.8	4.9	3.9			
Canada	76.3	81.7	5.3	2.1	7.6	3.3	7.1
Czech Republic	71.4	78.1	4.6	3.1	8.4	6.6	8.7
Denmark	74.2	79.0	4.2	3.4	7.3	3.3	5.3
Finland	73.8	81.0	3.7	3.1	14.7	2.4	4.4
France	75.0	82.5	4.3	3.3	6.5	4.2	5.5
Germany	74.7	80.7	4.5	3.6	9.3	6.4	9.6
Greece	75.5	80.6	6.2	4.4	3.9	4.0	6.3
Hungary	66.3	75.1	8.4	3.2	4.9	6.4	7.9
Iceland	77.5	81.4	2.4	3.4	14.2		
Ireland	**73.9**	**79.1**	**5.5**	**2.3**	**9.2**	**2.9**	**6.4**
Italy	75.3	81.6	5.1	6.0	4.5	4.5	7.2
Japan	77.1	84.0	3.4	1.9	7.8		
Korea	71.7	79.2		1.3	1.4	5.2	11.0
Luxembourg	74.7	81.2	4.6	3.1	7.1	5.7	
Mexico	72.8	77.3	25.9	1.8	1.1		
Netherlands	75.3	80.5	5.2	3.2	13.0	3.5	9.0
New Zealand	75.7	80.8	5.4	2.2	9.7		
Norway	75.6	81.1	3.9	2.9	10.3	3.1	6.0
Poland	68.8	77.5	8.9	2.2	4.9		
Portugal	72.0	79.1	5.6	3.2	3.7	3.3	7.3
Slovak Republic	69.0	77.0	8.3		7.3	5.9	
Spain	74.9	82.4	4.5	3.3	3.7		
Sweden	77.0	81.9	3.4	2.9	8.4	2.4	5.0
Switzerland	76.8	82.5	4.6	3.5		4.1	9.3
Turkey	66.1	70.7	40.3	1.3	1.1	2.2	5.4
United Kingdom	75.0	79.8	5.8	1.8	5.3	3.3	6.2
United States	73.9	79.4	7.1	2.8	8.3	3.0	5.9
Average of OECD countries[8]	73.9	80.0	7.1	2.9	7.1	4.2	7.0

1. Cross-country comparisons need to be interpreted with caution. See OECD *Health Data* 2002, Sources and Methods for details of methodology variations across country.
2. Data refer to 1997 for Italy; 1998 for Greece.
3. Data refer to 1998 for New Zealand.
4. Data refer to 1998 for Australia and France; 1999 for Denmark, Greece, Hungary, Iceland, Ireland, Sweden and Untied States.
5. Data refer to 1998 for Japan; 1999 for Denmark, Greece, Iceland, Italy, Sweden and United States.
6. Data refer to 1998 for Portugal; 1999 for Australia, Canada, Denmark, Greece and Italy.
7. Data refer to 1998 for Denmark, Greece, Italy and Portugal; 1999 for Australia, Canada, France and United States.
8. Unweighted average. Includes only available countries at the relevant point in time.

Source: OECD Health Data 2002.

Box 9. Private practice in public hospitals

The Irish healthcare system has a unique structure with a mixture of a universal public health service and a fee-based private system. About one-third of the population hold medical cards, which entitles them to all health services and medicines free of charge. Those without medical cards are also entitled to care in public beds at modest charges.[1] Despite the presence of a universal public health service, however, a large and increasing number of the Irish population – currently 45 per cent – hold private medical insurance, as private insurance is perceived to increase timeliness of care and choice of providers. The public and private sectors are entwined within all levels of the Irish health system as the same personnel may deliver public and private services within the same facilities. Those with private insurance generally receive "private" care in private or semi-private accommodation, and choose their own consultant, but a significant part of this private care is also delivered in public hospitals. There are incentives for doctors and hospital consultants to maximise the number of private patients, as they are paid on a capitation and salaried basis, respectively, for their service to the public patients, but are paid on a fee-for-service basis in dealing with the private patients. The Health (Amendment) Act 1991 designates about 20 per cent of beds in public hospitals as private. However, evidence indicates that 30 per cent of patients treated at acute public hospitals were private patients in 1999 and 2000 (Wiley, 2001).

1. The two-thirds of the population without medical cards must pay for their general practitioner care and up to a maximum of € 70 per month for medicines under the Drug Payment Scheme. In addition, they are entitled to care in public hospital beds on payment of a small per diem for a fixed number of days in any one year.

health care system. At the same time, to better inform public perceptions and to improve decisionmaking about priorities, greater transparency is required in relation to the existing distribution of resources within, and outputs of, the health services.

Weaknesses in the management and organisation of the health sector need to be addressed

Concerns have also been raised that inefficient management of existing hospital facilities and organisational problems contribute to difficulties in accessing services. Long waiting times for public hospitals have co-existed with large variations in the average length of stay among hospitals for the same type of procedure, suggesting that the problem might be alleviated by a more efficient management of available resources (Wiley, 2001). The findings of a value-for-money study commissioned for the health services indicate that there is large scope for improving management practices in the system.[54] In particular, more co-ordination across the ambulatory care sector and the inpatient care sector could help to achieve productivity gains and reduce the workload of hospitals.

As in many other OECD countries, Ireland has made efforts to introduce reforms to the hospital funding system in order to provide incentives for greater efficiency. Most Irish hospitals receive block budgets from regional health boards, which has provided few incentives for hospitals to improve the efficiency of their operations. In order to introduce financial incentives, a case-mix budget model, based on the Diagnostic Related Groups approach (DRGs), has been introduced to 32 acute general hospitals. The 2001 Health Strategy envisages a structured broadening of the case-mix budget model as a financial allocation tool for the hospital system.[55] In addition, increased transparency in determining funding allocations and other aspects of the funding process is being sought. The efforts in this direction should help create the incentives for better performance, but one particular difficulty in encouraging performance orientation is the poorly developed information systems in the Irish health sector as discussed above, which makes monitoring and evaluation very difficult. Priority should thus be given to developing a comprehensive health information system, in particular, through prioritising investments in IT infrastructure and training, to enhance transparency and accountability of the health system.

Concerns have also been raised about the large number of health boards and their governance structure. Arguments have been made that the current system is "over-governed" by ten health boards for a population of four million.[56] The lack of co-operation between health boards, for example, lack of shared services and unwillingness to share knowledge and experiences, has been seen as a limiting factor. The decisions of health boards also tend to be heavily influenced by local concerns which could adversely affect the efficient delivery of health services and lead to sub-specialisation of the hospital system. While the establishment of the Health Boards Executive in February 2002 should help to improve co-operation of health boards, the proposals calling for a smaller number of health boards deserve further investigation, along with the measures to improve their governance structure. Enhanced co-operation among health boards will also be essential for reaping the benefits from synergies and economies of scale. It would also help to ensure consistent application of service and quality standards nationwide.

Managing public infrastructure investment

Ireland faces an infrastructure deficit resulting from strong economic growth, which is putting public spending under significant pressure at the same time as related EU transfers are declining. A major public infrastructure investment programme has been launched under the National Development Plan (NDP) 2000-2006 to alleviate some of the infrastructure constraints (Table 10). The

Table 10. **Plan for investment in economic and social infrastructure under National Development Plan (NDP)**
2000-2006, million euros at constant 1999 prices

Sub-programme	ESIOP[1]	Regional operational programme[2]	Total
National roads	5 968		5 968
Non-national roads		2 032	2 032
Public transport – Greater Dublin Area	2 012		2 012
Regional public transport	825		825
Environmental services	3 212	1 359	4 571
Communications/Electronic commerce		152	152
Energy	185		185
Housing	7 618		7 618
Health	2 540		2 540
Urban and village renewal		131	131
Cultural, recreational and sports development		493	493
Seaports and regional airports		72	72
Total	22 360	4 239	26 599
Memorandum:			
Accumulative total as per cent of GNP in 1999	29.5	5.6	35.1

1. Refers to Economic and Social Infrastructure Operational Programme, The NDP consists of seven Operational Programmes including five inter-regional programmes. The ESIOP is the largest among them.
2. This column presents the sub-programmes of the two regional programmes that correspond to economic and social infrastructure.

Source: Department of Finance.

substantial increase in spending planned under the NDP seems to be justified to deal with the problem, but it is important to get the maximum mileage out of the increased spending.

The benefits, or returns, on public infrastructure investment are often hard to measure, making objective assessment of proposals for government investment very difficult. Much has been achieved in this area with the introduction of formal expenditure reviews and the systematic evaluations associated with EU funds, comprising *ex ante*, ongoing, mid-term and *ex post* evaluation with respect to the National Development Plan.[57] But the decline in the share of EU funds in overall investment should not lead to any weakening of this evaluation framework. Moreover, economic and cost-benefit analysis should be reinforced in all areas of public infrastructure investment, but these analyses themselves will need to be monitored closely as circumstances change. For Ireland, this is a particularly useful tool for the successful delivery of the National Development Plan. Including explicit *ex ante* processes for specifying, evaluating and financing large-scale investment projects, along with *ex post* oversight, should help reduce the risks of substantial costs overruns and inappropriate expenditures.

Final investment costs under the National Development Plan are estimated to be much higher than initially planned. The *ex ante* evaluation of the NDP had already raised concerns as to whether the economy has the capacity to absorb the planned level of infrastructure investment (CSF, 1999). The report found that the construction sector was already running into capacity constraints, particularly labour supply, and there was a possibility that this could hinder the ability to effectively deliver the increase in infrastructure investment aspired to in the Plan. Indeed, the cost of programmes under the NDP was estimated to have risen by 32 per cent between 1999 and 2001. In road construction, the estimated costs of the national road programme had soared from € 5.9 billion in 1999 to € 15.8 billion in 2002, due mainly to construction cost inflation, design changes, additional land acquisition costs, and under-estimation of project prices. The achievement of the ambitious targets set out under the NDP will likely hinge on the ability to overcome constraints in the construction sector and in the planning process generally. The project management of investment programmes will thus need to be considerably tightened up and planning issues tackled squarely.

One way to overcome the constraints in the construction sector could be to accelerate the efforts to increase the import content of construction services. Ireland has been active in advertising public procurement internationally (Table 11). In particular, the authorities have been increasing the size of projects being tendered in order to encourage large international firms to participate in infrastructure construction and have facilitated entry of their workers. Announcing

Table 11. **Share of public procurement being openly advertised internationally in European Union countries**[1]

Value of public procurement which is openly advertised in per cent of total value of public procurement

	1995	1996	1997	1998	1999	2000	2001
Austria	5	8	7	8	7	13	15
Belgium	7	8	11	14	16	16	19
Denmark	16	13	13	13	14	21	16
Finland	8	9	8	9	10	13	15
France	5	7	8	11	12	15	17
Germany	5	6	6	7	5	6	6
Greece	34	37	43	45	39	33	35
Ireland	**11**	**16**	**19**	**16**	**17**	**21**	**20**
Italy	10	10	11	11	13	18	15
Luxembourg	5	7	9	14	13	12	11
Netherlands	5	5	6	5	6	11	12
Portugal	15	18	15	16	15	15	18
Spain	9	11	11	12	17	25	23
Sweden	12	12	13	13	14	20	26
United Kingdom	15	15	17	16	15	22	21
Total EU	8	9	11	11	11	15	15

1. Value of public procurement published in the EU official journal as percentage of estimated total value of public procurement.

Source: Internal Market Directorate General, European Commission.

calls for tender internationally can also contribute to a greater efficiency of infrastructure spending by enhancing competition for public contracts. While Ireland has made much progress in this area, there is scope for further increasing competition through these means.

Ireland has embarked on the use of Public Private Partnerships (PPP) for priority infrastructure projects under the National Development Plan.[58] The Government believes that PPP embody significant potential for achieving accelerated delivery of strategic national infrastructure and quality public services on a long-term value-for-money basis. The PPP process is currently being explored on a pilot project basis to ensure "learning by doing." The first project – involving a bundle of five post-primary schools – was launched in July 2000. There are currently some 40 projects at various stages of procurement ranging from roads to environmental services, public transport and third-level education. Projects are also being developed in the courts and non-acute hospital services sectors. An additional benefit from PPP could be the possibility of introducing a rational charging scheme, and the authorities will also need to explore the introduction of appropriate pricing mechanisms on the use of infrastructure, *e.g.* toll charges on roads.

The use of PPP can be an effective tool for promoting efficiency and improving the delivery of certain public goods. However, results in other OECD countries have not been uniformly positive.[59] Some of the privately funded infrastructure projects can entail large liabilities, both explicit and contingent, for future years, which are not reflected in the budget. Thus PPP initiatives need to be carefully designed, and Ireland will need to follow international best practices to avoid potential problems. Minimising the fiscal risks and ensuring value-for-money will depend in part on the scope for prudent selection of projects and a competitive procurement process. In particular, the appraisal procedures in place to determine that PPP is the best value option should be rigorously applied. The experience of other countries suggests that most efficiency gains stem from the permanent exposure of potential contractors to competition, rather than from the tender as such. It is therefore essential that the process of tendering and contracting be organised in such a way that they limit the government's dependence on the incumbent franchise or concession holder.[60]

Agenda for future reform

The previous sections suggest that there is considerable scope for improvement in the management of public expenditure in Ireland. Given the upward pressure on spending and the prospect of slowing fiscal revenues, it is essential that Ireland push ahead quickly with a comprehensive reform to better control public spending and to raise the efficiency and quality of expenditure. An agenda for such reform is presented in this section and specific policy recommendations are summarised in Box 10.

Box 10. Summary of recommendations

Reform the institutional arrangements for budgeting

- Adopt a top-down budgeting approach, so that the Government makes a binding political decision as to the level of total expenditures and divides them among broad expenditure areas before approving detailed expenditure plans.
- Develop and extend the multi-annual budget envelope.

Move toward results-focused public management

- Accelerate efforts to move to results-focused budgeting and management.
- Include both *ex ante* and *ex post* performance indicators in budget documents (departmental Spending Estimates).
- Introduce more flexible human resource management, including greater use of open recruitment and competitive promotions.

Strengthen the accountability framework

- Accelerate efforts to develop the Management Information Framework.
- Strengthen evaluation and value-for-money audits in all spending areas.
- Increase the oversight role of the Parliament and the Comptroller and Auditor General.

Enhance the role of market-based provision and other allocation mechanisms

- Make more use of market mechanisms in publicly funded services, including a wider use of contracting-out and benchmarking.
- Make an extended use of price signals, in particular, in higher education and the health sector.
- Extend competitive tendering and Public Private Partnerships (PPP), taking a prudent approach.

Reform the funding system of local governments and their spending responsibilities

- Consider giving local authorities powers to levy local property taxes.
- Use *ex ante* estimation of standard costs and increase co-financing of ear-marked grants by local authorities.
- Move towards block grants for those projects without spillover effects, while making continued efforts to improve the distribution formula.
- Enhance co-operation and co-ordination between local authorities and between national/local authorities and other public bodies.
- Consider mergers/transfer of functions to streamline institutional framework at sub-national level.

Reforming the institutional arrangements for budgeting

The increasing spending pressure in the environment of slowing revenues highlights the need for further enhanced aggregate spending control, while continuing to better align strategic priorities and budget allocation. In this regard, the authorities should continue moving to a top-down approach to budget formulation, in which the Government makes a binding political decision as to the level of total expenditures and divides them among broad expenditure areas according to strategic priorities. This would allow the Department of Finance to largely withdraw from the details of budgetary allocations for each department and instead focus on providing strategic guidance on spending priorities to departments. In addition, the current medium-term budget framework could be extended further by implementing the rolling multi-annual expenditure "envelope" system. This would allow each spending Department to freely reallocate resources among its various agencies and programmes under a medium-term hard budget constraint. The recent move to a multi-annual framework for capital investment is welcome as essential investment projects would be insulated from *ad hoc* budgetary cuts.

Prioritisation of spending could also be facilitated by stepping up the ongoing efforts for systematic expenditure reviews. The framework for regular and comprehensive programme review should be established but, given the past experience, it is likely to require a more systematic guidance from the centre. In addition, the introduction of sunset clauses to new programmes should help move resources away from the programmes that no longer serve the original objectives, and also ensure that programmes are regularly reviewed.

Moving toward results-focused public management

The government should follow through with the Strategic Management Initiative (SMI) to move from its traditional system of input-focused management and budgeting toward one centred on outputs and outcomes. The adoption of a more top-down budgeting process and a multi-annual budgeting envelope would empower individual departments to choose the most efficient mix of inputs to carry out their activities within a pre-set limit, which could lead to significant efficiency gains. In return for the certainty involved in multi-annual allocations, the departments involved in running the programmes should contract to deliver outputs according to agreed standards. In order to shift the focus of the policy formulation and budgetary review processes from inputs to outputs and outcomes, the government will also need to take steps to systematically integrate output indicators into the budgetary and policy-making process. The government's recent decision to publish the results of all future expenditure reviews is an important step in this direction. Both *ex ante* indicators in the form of goals and *ex post* indicators as a means of verifying performance will need to be integrated into budget documents (departmental Spending Estimates) to show the effectiveness of alternative programmes. This would also enhance transparency and serve to make budgetary institutions more accountable.

Decentralisation of the personnel management function and increased flexibility in the public service will be essential for an efficient delivery of public service. Concerted efforts are needed to change the existing human resource management practices by increasing devolution and accountability and by introducing stronger links between performance and reward/recognition/promotion. In this regard, implementation of the current plans for a modernisation of human resource management practices should be accelerated, setting deadlines and clearly linking public sector pay increases to the modernisation of the public service.

Strengthening the accountability framework

The efforts to strengthen accountability for performance or results should accompany the move toward more flexible and results-focussed budgeting and management, but it will also require developing measurable performance indicators. The ongoing efforts to develop the Management Information Framework (MIF) need to be stepped up to support enhanced decision-making, performance and accountability. Greater weight should be given to developing effective value-for-money audit and systematic evaluations of programme and projects. In this regard, there is scope for strengthening the role of the Parliament and the Comptroller and Auditor General in results-oriented auditing and reviewing control mechanisms. Currently the role of the Public Accounts Committee is focused on accountability for inputs. Its role, and that of other committees, could be developed to include greater emphasis on outputs, and possibly outcomes. Strengthening the accountability for results would also require expanding the role of the Comptroller and Auditor General in value-for-money audits.

Enhancing the role of market-based provision and other allocation mechanisms

Enhancing the role of market-based provision and other allocation mechanisms could boost the allocative efficiency of public expenditure. Many OECD countries have found it useful to make greater use of market-type instruments in certain aspects of publicly funded services. The techniques that have been tried include user charges, benchmarking, vouchers, creating internal competition and contracting-out. Some of these market mechanisms have been increasingly used in Ireland, but there is still large room for extending their use. In particular:

- A wider use of contracting-out could be made for the central and local government activities which have a large potential for cost reductions and improvement in the quality of the services provided.
- A wider use of benchmarking techniques should be pursued as a means for evaluating and improving the management and delivery

systems in the public service. In particular, benchmarking could be a particularly useful tool in providing performance indicators and disseminating best practices in the health and education sector as well as in local government.

- An extended use of price signals could reduce excessive demand for costly public provision. Introducing water charges would make consumers more cost conscious and also ease the pressure on expenditure. Given high rates of private return to tertiary education, third-level fees could be re-introduced, accompanied by means-testing mechanisms and loan arrangements. In the healthcare sector, measures can be taken to further increase or introduce user charges. In increasing user charges, great care will need to be taken to avoid poverty traps associated with means-testing.
- Competitive tendering and public-private partnerships are set to be expanded further, in particular, in the context of the delivery of the National Development Plan. But contracts will need to be designed carefully to allow for an appropriate sharing of the risks associated with such major projects, and more emphasis will need to be placed on regulation and on providing the right frameworks and incentives.

Reforming the funding system of local governments and their spending responsibilities

Improving the effectiveness of spending by sub-national governments should be a key element of public expenditure management reform. While pursuing the ongoing efforts to improve the quality of performance management system at local level, reform should aim at providing greater flexibility and responsibilities to local authorities and increasing the share of funding which is locally levied. Given the relatively narrow range of functions assigned to local authorities, local government in Ireland has significant scope for development through the devolution of functions from central government or transfer of functions from other public bodies. A thorough review of spending and financing responsibilities across government layers will be needed to make decentralisation an effective means to enhance the effectiveness of public spending. Serious consideration should also be given to raising local revenues by re-introducing local property taxes on residential housing, which has many advantages as a sub-national tax. Introducing a local property tax could help enhance the accountability of elected representatives, as local residents will be bearing the cost of local services. In addition, property tax is less volatile than other taxes. Such reform would widen the tax raising competencies of local governments so as to achieve a higher degree of congruence between revenue and spending responsibilities.

The use of earmarked grants should be confined to those projects where the benefits extend substantially outside the area of a local authority. One option to improve the efficiency of spending through earmarked grants might be to have their allocation based on *ex ante* estimation of standard costs instead of *ex post* actual costs. With increased taxing power, some co-financing of earmarked grants by local authorities could be expanded, which should help to contain cost pressures. Many small grants could also be merged into a broader envelope with key strategic objectives, which would give more flexibility to local authorities on how to achieve them. Other services which do not have clear spillover effects should be funded by block grants, which will allow local governments more freedom to organise the expenditure programmes. At the same time, the current effort to improve the distribution formula of the Local Government Fund should continue to be pursued so as to make the Fund the main instrument for ensuring horizontal equity between jurisdictions.

There is also scope for reducing inefficiencies arising from the small size of some local authorities, and from limited co-ordination between local authorities and between national/local authorities and other public service agencies. Given the plethora of public sector bodies at local or regional level, enhancing the level of co-ordination will be particularly important to achieve effective planning and delivery of services. Efforts should also be made to internalise spillovers of local services via co-operation between local authorities or public bodies and the merging of the small local authorities.

IV. Sustaining growth: the structural policy dimensions

Introduction

The future prosperity of the Irish economy will continue to hinge on sustained business investment and an increase in the well-educated labour force, accompanied by a higher participation rate. The availability of these productive factors depends, among others, on the likely evolution of the cost of living in Ireland, which is already among the highest in the EU. To mitigate the rise in the cost of living, and also to improve welfare, it is essential to advance regulatory reform in the sheltered sector of the economy, which would promote productivity gains and weaken the pricing power of the incumbent firms. At the same time, success in implementing the official strategy to seek higher value-added in investment will depend on how many high-skilled workers and researchers Ireland can provide or attract. In this regard, it is important to address the issues that are facing higher education institutions, while improving human capital in the workplace. Increasing labour supply is also a key to maintaining soundness of public finance in the long run. Continuing economic growth should also be environmentally sustainable. This chapter examines various structural policy issues related to sustainability. A summary of recommendations from previous Surveys and the Regulatory Reform Review is provided in Table 12, along with assessment of progress and new recommendations.

Improving regulation and promoting competition and market solutions

While the international comparative indicators suggest that Ireland has an overall light regulatory burden, regulatory problems associated with weak competition policy and unfinished pro-market regulatory regimes has left a legacy of policy which is oriented to the interests of service providers rather than consumers.[61] For instance, inflation pressure led the government to temporarily control beer prices in 2001, and in 2002 concern about a rising trend in employer and public liability claims led to a regulation banning solicitors from potentially claim-inducing advertising. In both instances more suitable market solutions were available. The needed transformation was outlined in the OECD's *Review of Regulatory Reform in*

Table 12. **Implementing structural reform – an overview of progress**

Previous survey's recommendations	Action taken since 2001	Assessment/recommendations
I. The tax system		
– Reduce the marginal income tax rates to improve incentives to work, particularly for women	The standard rate band widened further.	Marginal tax rate has become reasonably low. Review pre-retirement allowance, which distorts incentive to work for elderly.
– Reduce the standard corporate tax rate	Unified corporate tax rate has been reduced from 16 per cent to 12½ per cent since January 2003.	Reduction of tax rate has been achieved on schedule.
II. The benefit and wage formation systems		
– Soften the impact of the introduction of national minimum wage on employment and incentives to attend the school	The national minimum wage was increased from Ir£4.4 to 4.7 in July 2001 and to 5 in October 2002.	Impact is negligible despite the subsequent rises given that the level was not high. Future adjustment should be prudent as average wage growth becomes moderate.
III. Active labour market policies		
– Curtail the existing make-work programme	Community Employment Scheme has been phased down.	More substantial downsizing will be required.
– Focus on targeted employment subsidy programmes	The eligibility for Back to Work Allowance scheme has been tightened, limiting its support to the long-term unemployed.	A welcome step.
– Limiting the targets of training programmes to avoid dead-weight	Emphasis is now placed on life-long leaning, including basic literacy for older cohort and education for early school leavers.	The shift of focus on vulnerable groups is reasonable.
IV. Enhance product market competition		
– Give the competition authority independent power to review mergers. The independence of the authority should be strengthened with respect to the appointment and budget.	Responsibility of deciding on mergers has passed from DETE to the competition authority since January 2003. The authority will also be able to undertake its own recruitment.	A welcome step forward.
– Continue to develop an all Ireland electricity market and to enforce divestiture of some generating capacity of the dominant company.	Market opening for non-households is being extended as a step toward full liberalisation in 2005. The third auction of Virtual Independent Power Producers (VIPP) was conducted in 2002 and 60 per cent of eligible users switched suppliers.	Full liberalisation should proceed by 2005 as planned. Ensure the continued installation of new generating capacity through the creation of a power exchange. Separate generation and transmission by the incumbent. Break up the generating capacity of the incumbent into competing units.

Table 12. **Implementing structural reform – an overview of progress** (*cont.*)

Previous survey's recommendations	Action taken since 2001	Assessment/recommendations
– Promote competition in telecommunication	The independent regulator has been established since 2001. Local Loop Unbundling has been introduced since April 2002 though with considerable delay.	Strengthen the power of the regulator.
– Remove entry barriers	Restrictions on the entry to retail pharmacies have been largely removed since early 2002. Easing restrictions on liquor licensing is being considered.	Remaining entry conditions for pharmacists trained outside the country should be removed. The process of easing restrictions on liquor licensing should be accelerated. Further reform is needed in legal services.
V. Alleviating the housing constraint		
– Broaden the rental market	A commission report was published in 2000 but no substantial progress has been made since then.	The process should be accelerated.
– Reduce tax incentive for speculative investment on properties. Increase opportunity cost of holding undeveloped land.	Interest deductibility on borrowing by investors has been reintroduced.	Promote supply of undeveloped land further.
VI. Improve public sector efficiency (see chapter III as well)		
– Pursue modernisation of public services through implementing Strategic Management Initiatives (SMI) and introducing regulatory impact assessment (RIA).	SMI has been implemented in number of areas, though it had not affected the dynamics governing the evolution of policy. The government plans to introduce RIA to the policy process.	Public management needs to be further reoriented toward output and outcomes rather than controlling spending. Need rigorous project assessment in general government measures to introduce RIA.

Source: OECD.

Ireland, 2001, and many of the proposals have been taken up in governmental programmes covering regulatory and administrative reform and in measures to liberalise several economic sectors. This section reviews the outstanding policy issues against the background of recent initiatives.

The administrative and regulatory system

At the highest level of reform is the Strategic Management Initiative (SMI) and the associated civil service modernisation programme (see Chapter III). The objective is the provision "of services to the public which are both excellent in quality and effective in delivery". Although a great deal has been achieved in making the civil service more open, transparent and accountable, further work remains to be done. As noted in Chapter III, implementation has been particularly slow with respect to human resource management and information systems management that are needed to redirect public management toward output and outcomes rather than simply controlling the use of funds. More efficient public spending will also require the establishment of such a system.

Reform of the *ad hoc* regulatory system remains on the policy agenda. Some of the problems in the current system have been highlighted by the courts which have had to rule in a number of areas (taxis, pharmacies, telecommunications and very nearly in electricity where the grid operator threatened to challenge the due process of the regulator in court). The government has committed to publishing a National Policy Statement (or White Paper) in 2003, which will establish a set of core principles to guide future regulation and regulatory management. The government also intends to introduce regulatory impact assessment (RIA) to the policy process. A key finding of the OECD review of Ireland's regulatory regime was that current systems and capacity for assessing and reporting on the likely implications of proposed regulations need to be strengthened. A Working Group was formed and has developed a draft RIA model specifically for the Irish context, which has been submitted to the government with a view to piloting the model in a number of government departments. Pressures for change will strengthen when the European Commission adopts RIA in its policy making process, and in an important move the administration is now required to present to the Legislature an assessment of the impact of EU legislation on Ireland.

The previous *Survey* highlighted examples of inadequate regulation in a number of sectors including transport, pharmacies, pubs and the legal profession. Recent experience appears to confirm continuing weakness in the regulatory process, with the court system often having to take the lead in resolving what are essentially regulatory issues (*e.g.* in inter-city buses). Pharmacies present a useful example. Although location restrictions were removed in January 2002, it remains the case that pharmacists trained outside the country can now only operate a pharmacy that has been running for more than three years.

Another aspect of the reform process which is potentially very important is the proposed National Policy Statement on Regulation. The government called for public submissions which are now being assessed. The intention is to formulate a policy statement which will set down principles for the regulatory system. To move away from the traditional focus on producer interests, the principles should anchor the regulatory system in competition policy, a key recommendation of the OECD's *Review of Regulatory Reform in Ireland*.

Competition policy and enforcement

From the beginning of this year competition policy and enforcement has taken an important step forward. The responsibility for examining and deciding mergers and take-overs has been transferred from the Ministry of Enterprise, Trade and Employment (DETE) to the Competition Authority, and cases must be decided on the basis of competition criteria alone. The authority has now achieved greater autonomy and will be able to undertake their own recruitment. The previous *survey* noted deficiencies in enforcement but there have been important improvements. Since July 2002 the authority has a leniency programme that is agreed with the prosecution to encourage parties to make first-hand disclosures which are necessary to prove secret agreements. This possibility is important in view of the new cartel law which has been in force since July 2002. The new law has introduced punishments of up to 5 years in prison. A new office of corporate enforcement has been established and the police have now been officially brought into this body. Judges are also now being upskilled in the relevant complexities. Procedures for covering white collar crime including improved co-ordination with other bodies are being reviewed. The Competition Authority has also been active in its advocacy role presenting its opinions regarding, *inter alia*, transport, electricity and telecommunications. In sum, a great deal has been achieved in redressing the weaknesses noted in the last *survey* and in the *Regulatory Reform Review*. It is now up to other players to adapt to the new approach to competition which represents an important change of course for Ireland.

Telecommunications: establishing a low cost regime

With its location and emphasis on high technology industries, Ireland is more than usually dependent on creating an efficient telecommunications sector for both domestic and overseas services. An indication of the importance is that the Irish government guaranteed the contract to build a trans-Atlantic optical fibre connection to ensure that Ireland was connected to the high capacity system. Although service prices have fallen significantly since the liberalisation began at the end of 1998 and are relatively favourable, mobile prices for post-paid subscribers remain relatively high, reflecting the fact that for a long time there were only two service providers with the third licence in court. Despite this Ireland has a good mobile penetration rate that compares well with EU countries, but the use of secure servers is lagging. Limited availability of broadband services is also an issue with small enterprises. Delivery of leased lines by the incumbent has been slow.

These features in part reflect the difficulty of establishing a competitive market in a small economy, but that should not be an excuse for not making further progress. A problem was the weak enforcement powers included in the original Act establishing the regulator, which has been strengthened by the 2002 Act. The situation was compounded by the decision to use a beauty contest plus fees, that resulted from the consultation with the government and the European Commission in the allocation of 2G mobile licenses. The allotment decision was legally challenged, resulting in lengthy delays, which reduced competition in the mobile market. Like incumbents in a number of other countries, Eircom has also taken the regulator to court thereby deterring potential competitors.

The regulator has made use of price caps in both the mobile and the fixed line segment. In the latter, the intention is to force the incumbent to improve efficiency. But price caps have recently been raised to higher levels (CPI minus zero) and sub-caps have been dropped. To support competition the regulator has adopted the technique of "co-mingling"[62] as part of collocation policy to give competitors access to the local loop: 40 exchanges are already unbundled and by next year the number is expected to be 100 exchanges covering about 50 per cent of lines.[63] This pace is, however, rather slow compared with most other EU members. Three 3G licenses were granted. They are subject to "roll-out" requirements and infrastructure sharing is allowed to a limited extent. The sharing of mast sites is allowed in the development of 3G networks following decisions taken in a number of other countries to reduce the costs of 3G roll-out while ensuring that competition is not jeopardised.

The Communications Regulation Act, enacted in April 2002, established a Commission in place of a single Director as a regulator. The Commission has been given the ability to impose more severe fines if there is a criminal conviction. But it cannot impose high administrative fines, which lessens its ability to put pressure on the incumbent. The regulatory environment is about to change with a new law to bring the system into line with the EU directive. The basis will be the competition framework so that markets are to be defined and *ex ante* regulation applied to the relevant market segment. Market dominance (in the context of anti-abuse cases) is to be defined as 40-50 per cent of market share rather than the 25 per cent which has been used as a rule of thumb up till now.

Electricity: establishing competition in a small market

The small size of the market and the distance[64] to alternative suppliers represents a particular challenge to establishing an efficient market for electricity.

The regulatory issues were thus always going to remain difficult. While the Electricity Supply Board (ESB) has remained a vertically integrated company, its business units are being separated, with the establishment of an independent transmission system operator known as EirGrid. However, the separation of transmission and dispatch functions from ESB has led to a series of disputes concerning the distribution of responsibilities between ESB and the EirGrid. As a result of the agreement, EirGrid is responsible for operating as a wholly separate entity, though transmission system ownership remains with ESB. EirGrid can also give a preliminary design of transmission expansion to ESB and has the right to veto final designs done by ESB, though the construction work is carried out by ESB. Such arrangements where the operator is separate from the owner can work well and act to prevent the over-building of the transmission system that can occur when ownership and operation are in the same hand. On the other hand, there is a risk that the incumbent can influence the transmission system to its advantage. Therefore, the government should monitor and amend, if necessary, the current arrangements for separation of the operation and ownership of the grid to ensure that the objectives of an efficient and secure grid are not compromised (OECD, 2001c).

The challenge for the regulator is to establish a market mechanism even though the number of actual and potential competitors is small and to ensure the continued installation of new generating capacity and improvements of the national grid (bottlenecks are often of a regional nature). In the absence of divestiture of generating capacity by ESB, the options are limited. To be economic, any new generating capacity would probably need to be at least 400 Mega watts, about 8 per cent of total capacity, but some third of the eligible market. With future gas and electricity prices uncertain (prices are still capped), it appears that new generators would face difficulties in raising finance for their projects. The current trading arrangements, where there is no electricity market (spot or future) but rather bilateral contracts with customers, does not offer generators the relative security and liquidity that a single buyer or a power pool system might. These issues are being addressed in the overall review of trading arrangements now being undertaken by the Commission for Electricity Regulation (CER). In the meantime, with competition on the generating side limited, the regulator has set out to control the behaviour of ESB through license conditions and by the establishment of "virtual independent power producers", VIPP.[65] A large proportion of power generated by ESB is auctioned to VIPPs who can then resell to their clients. In the view of the regulator, this system gives experience to some firms (VIPP) about how to market electricity and it also gives eligible users the experience with seeking out best deals. To date 36 per cent of the 1 600 eligible clients have switched "supplier" and one VIPP is going ahead with its own generating capacity. However, 23 per cent of the users that have switched have moved to the VIPP owned by the ESB, so that only a discount is effectively involved.[66]

The Policy Direction issued by the Minister for Public Enterprise in 1999 required that a review of the overall trading arrangements take place in 2004. This review will cover many aspects of the trading regime, including the nature of the trading system, obligation of supply, methods for calculating market prices and so on. The CER decided to accelerate this review expecting its completion within 2003. The decision is welcome and the review should provide a clear and coherent set of long-term market rules for trading to remove the current uncertainty from the market.

Transport: introducing competition and independent regulation

In recent years measures to promote competition and improve regulation in the public transport sector have been proposed in a number of government consultation papers.[67] Following elections in the summer of 2002, the newly appointed Minister for Transport announced his reform proposals for the public transport sector, which could result in the most radical overhaul of public transport in Ireland in many years. The reform package includes a dismantling of State-owned company CIÉ and transforming its three subsidiaries – Dublin Bus, Bus Éireann and Iarnród Éireann (Irish Rail) – into independent State companies with commercially focused boards. It is expected that the three companies will compete with each other in certain markets, as well as with companies in the private sector. At the same time, the government proposes to create an independent regulator of public transport. It is proposed that the independent regulator will have responsibility for procuring and regulating all public transport services and will also have responsibility for the allocation of all capital and current funding for public transport from the Exchequer. The government also plans to introduce "controlled competition" into the Dublin bus market. The plan is not to deregulate the bus market in the greater Dublin area, but to introduce competition in the form of franchising of routes or groups of routes. It is proposed that from the beginning of 2004, Dublin Bus will face competition up to 25 per cent of its network and that further routes will be franchised out over the coming years.

In the aviation sector, a new Commission for Aviation Regulation was established on a statutory basis in February 2001, which is responsible, among others, for regulating airport charges, approving arrangements for ground handling services, and licensing Irish airlines under EU licensing regulations. The plans to bring more competition into the operation of Dublin Airport and two regional (Shannon and Cork) airports are also being considered by the Government. A new government programme provides for the examination of proposals for an additional, privately owned, terminal at Dublin Airport. In order to test the viability of this project, the Government requested interested parties to submit "expressions of interest" to the Department of Transport by 31 October 2002. A panel has been set up to examine the fourteen submissions and to advise the Government on whether it should sanction a new terminal. The report of the Assessment Panel, published in March 2003, concluded that the development of an independently funded and operated terminal is both operationally and technically feasible, though it may not be financially viable with the existing level of aeronautical charges. The government also intends to continue transformation of State-owned Aer Rianta that operates airports, and, as part of this process, will ensure that Shannon and Cork Airports have greater autonomy, in the hope that this might introduce competition between regional airports.

Changing focus of industrial policy

Irish industrial policy is changing its focus away from production activities towards research and innovation activities in an attempt to move up the value chain (Dorgan, 2002). One of the reasons for this strategic change is the re-engineering of value chains due to increased globalisation and technological advances, which have changed when and where value is added along the chain. Another reason is the erosion of Ireland's previous advantages in areas such as low costs and plentiful labour as well as the emergence of new competitors, especially the acceding EU countries who are replicating Ireland's previous advantages. The authorities are encouraging the development of innovative activities by companies already operating in Ireland as well as seeking new emerging investors. Given the "critical mass" of FDI established, additional potential contribution is likely to come from the already established companies on top of that from new FDI.

The change in strategy will mean switching the emphasis from individual projects to the development of "clusters of excellence" in which technology companies, education and research activities, venture capital providers etc. interact and form a network to create a climate of innovation and entrepreneurship. These activities should integrate both indigenous and foreign firms' resources, thereby closing some of the previous partitions that have existed in the past.

It is also clear that, the success of this new strategy will depend on the quality of Ireland's human capital and its ability to foster this new innovation and research orientation. In this regard, the IDA has formed a new division: ESR (Education Skills and Research). Working closely with Science Foundation Ireland (SFI), the ESR is intended to facilitate the creation of an environment for new knowledge-based activity, that is, promoting the R&D and innovation capacity of the economy. This together with existing schemes such as the Programme for Research in Third Level Institutions should improve and accelerate Ireland's overall capacity to carry out high quality scientific research and therefore deepen its human capital.

Priorities in human capital development

The educational attainment of the labour force in Ireland has increased rapidly, as shown by the rapid rise in the share of population with at least upper-secondary education for younger cohorts, compared with older cohorts (Figure 14).

Figure 14. **Educational attainment of the working-age population**

Population with at least an upper-secondary qualification, 2001[1]

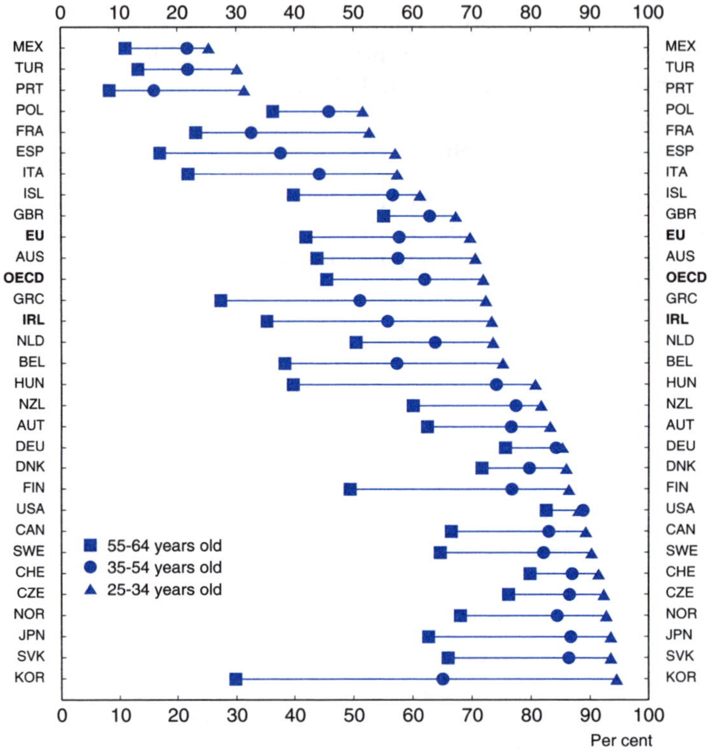

1. Per cent of each age group; 2000 for Austria, Belgium, Denmark, Hungary, the Netherlands and Norway.

Source: OECD, Labour Market Statistics database.

The upgrading of education and skill levels among the population, which has been one of the main contributors to Ireland's economic growth, will continue to remain important. In particular, the success of Ireland's current industrial strategy that envisages a repositioning towards knowledge-intensive, and high-technology activities will depend critically on the supply of high skilled workers and researchers. Demographic trends, however, indicate a substantial decline in numbers of secondary school leavers over this decade in Ireland, which will make it all the more important to increase enrolment and retention rates. In particular, Ireland's relatively low ranking among OECD countries in respect of mature age participation in higher education has been identified as an area to be tackled. The government has set the targets for substantial enrolment increases for this type of student, as part of the strategy to encourage lifelong learning.[68] Ireland's tertiary education also faces the challenge of increasing the numbers of post-graduate students and those on post-experience professional programmes, where Ireland tends to lag behind other countries. Strengthening research capacity at tertiary education institutions will also be important. The government has started to move in this direction. In particular, the National Development Plan (NDP) includes planned spending of € 698 million for a major investment programme aimed at enhancing research and development in higher education. More systematic efforts will however be needed to address the current weakness in technology transfer and commercialisation of research results, through an improved co-operation between business and higher education institutions.

The trend for rising secondary school completion has continued with increased attention being devoted to vocational education in the upper and post secondary level. But there is still some room for improvement, as the completion of upper-secondary education in Ireland is behind a number of other OECD countries. It is estimated that by the age of seventeen approximately 20 per cent of young Irish people have dropped out of education. While the factors that contribute to the problem of school dropouts are complex, poor economic status of the dropouts remains one major reason. The new Government elected in June 2002 has committed to continuing the efforts to combat early school leaving and address the needs of those who are disadvantaged at both primary and secondary level. The current objective is to retain 90 per cent of students to completion of senior-cycle secondary education.[69] A number of initiatives, including the Early School Leavers Initiative and the Stay in School Retention Initiative, have been undertaken under the School Competition Programme. The funding for the Programme was increased from € 2.4 million in 1998 to € 23 million in 2003, and € 23 million per annum has been committed over the next two years to August 2005. Legislative reform has also underpinned the current efforts. The Education Welfare Act 2000 provides a statutory framework to deal with the problems of school non-attendance, early school leaving and poor educational attainment among primary and secondary students. The Act also provides for the raising of the minimum school leaving age from fifteen to sixteen years, or the completion of three years of junior cycle education, whichever is the later. The Department of Education and Science currently operates a wide range of programmes aimed at enhancing access to and participation in education at all levels. The increased funding in this area is a move in the right direction, but it will be equally important to continually evaluate the effectiveness of these programmes. In addition, more needs to be done in the area of socio-educational programmes having strong outreach to disadvantaged families and communities.

With regard to the policy for improving human capital at work, emphasis is now placed on lifelong learning and encouraging business investment in training. A task force was established under the Programme for Prosperity and Fairness to develop a strategic framework for lifelong learning. It identified several priority measures including setting out the national framework of qualifications, ensuring basic skills for all, disseminating information, improving delivery and access, and providing better learning opportunities in the workplace. Among these priorities, ensuring basic literacy and numeracy skills for everyday life is particularly important as these skills are significantly low among older cohorts due to under-investment in education in the 1950s and the 1960s.[70] To address this problem, the budget appropriation to improve adult education increased from € 1 million in 1997 to € 25 million in 2002, with a corresponding increase in the number of beneficiaries from 5 000 in 1997 to 18 862 in 2001. There has also been some movement towards allowing employed early leavers to obtain the certificate on a part-time basis. Such a flexible arrangement for obtaining the certificates, together with an effort to let undereducated workers acquire a recognisable qualification through training schemes, would help reduce their vulnerability to an economic downturn, though the efficiency of re-training needs to be checked.

While multinational companies are active in training their employees, smaller firms tend to invest less in training, raising concerns about the continuing dualistic structure of the Irish economy as a whole. To address these concerns, the government has recently shifted its policy focus from predominantly firm-specific training initiatives to more horizontal approaches. The "Skillnets" training networks were set up in November 1998 to allow companies to formulate joint training courses that fit their needs. This initiative aims at encouraging small companies to invest more in training through joint training schemes that would meet their common needs while requiring lower costs than each company organising them individually.[71] Since 1999, 40 sector-based networks and 20 research networks have been established and over 2 300 companies have been involved in the programme. The network has been successful in encouraging the participation of small and medium-sized enterprises (SMEs) with 73 per cent of the companies in the programme having less than 50 employees.

Labour market policy

Ireland has traditionally spent a relatively large amount of funds on labour-market policy measures. However, with current low levels of unemployment, their role has changed radically. Given a significant labour shortage especially for skilled workers, a particular emphasis has been placed on encouraging the supply of labour from among women and older people. However, with the pressure on the labour market easing, measures to help the unemployed find jobs begin to regain importance, and the immigration policy is shifting towards greater selectivity.

Encouraging participation of female and older workers

The contribution of rising participation rates to the expansion of labour force weakened significantly in 2000 and 2001. Although the participation rate rose relatively rapidly in 2002, this may need to be discounted as it can be largely explained by some *ad hoc* factors such as a sharp rise in employment in the education and health sector. Against these backgrounds, FAS (2002) suggests that the recent moderation in participation rate may reflect an end of the past rapid trend in female participation rate, which rose from 36.5 per cent to 47.9 per cent during the period 1995 to 2000. However, as the female participation rate in Ireland is still much lower than Nordic and Anglo-Saxon countries, there is some room for raising it further through appropriate policy measures.

Significant efforts have been made in reducing the tax disincentives to work. As a result, tax wedges, defined as the gap between the real labour compensation perceived by employers and the real take-home pay, has continued to narrow over the past decade by some 3 to 4 percentage points. It is currently substantially lower than the OECD average. The replacement rate, the ratio of the unemployed income to the income at work, is also generally modest in Ireland.[72] Moreover, relatively high marginal tax rates, which were imposed particularly on lower income earners, have declined significantly as a result of the tax changes since 1998.[73] Those who receive income just above the tax exemption limits used to face 40 per cent of effective marginal tax rate under the marginal relief[74], but their net effective marginal tax rate has been reduced to zero by increased standard tax credits that eliminate their tax liabilities. Participation of women has also been facilitated by a move towards widening the standard rate band and placing it on a per person basis in recent years, as well as by lower tax rates. On the other hand, disincentives to work arise from the possible loss of child dependent allowances for those moving to work. To alleviate this problem, the government has shifted financial resources from child dependent allowances to child benefit, which is available irrespective of employment status of the parents. However, neutralising the tax incentive to work in this way incurs a deadweight loss as parents already in the workforce can also benefit from this scheme. Setting certain eligibility condition would reduce the budgetary cost but at the same time introduce the problem of a poverty trap.

Since much has already been done to reduce tax disincentives toward work, policy to encourage female participation needs to focus more on facilitating flexible working arrangements and expanding childcare facilities. Although the government has moved along these lines by passing the laws on career leave and the protection of part-time workers, there is a significant scope for further development as only 7 per cent of firms allow career breaks and only 13 per cent firms adopted flexible time systems (FAS, 2002). Childcare facilities should also be expanded in line with the National Development Plan, which sets the target of increasing childcare places by 30 per cent between 2000 and 2003. Furthermore, policies to address the shortage of houses near workplaces and the bottlenecks in transportation capacity are also quite important as both of these problems could discourage the participation of second earners by lengthening the commuting time.

As for the financial disincentive for the participation of older workers, the past study suggested that implicit tax rates on continued work embedded in benefits for the elderly are also low in Ireland among the OECD countries (Blondal and Scarpetta, 1997). The participation rate of older workers, currently 46.4 per cent, is much higher than the average of 38 per cent for all EU countries, and it still continues to rise further, cohort effect outweighing age affect. Unlike other EU countries, encouraging older workers to remain in workplaces may not face resistance by their younger peers as the labour market is relatively tight in Ireland. In this respect, the *Pre-Retirement Allowance* has even become counter productive as it was introduced during the period of much higher unemployment.

Active labour market policy: employing the unemployed

Despite the substantial reduction in unemployment, Ireland still retains a large number and scale of the active labour market policy (ALMP) measures. In 2002, the number of participants in the ALMP schemes is almost equal to that of the unemployed as defined by the ILO (Table 13). Although ALMP measures may alleviate the labour shortage by helping the unemployed people back to work, their effectiveness and efficiency need to be checked closely.

The Irish ALMP schemes consist of four major components: general training, specific skills training, direct employment schemes and provision of employment subsidies. As in many other OECD countries, empirical studies assessing the impact of these schemes suggest that direct employment schemes show no statistically significant effect on the chances to find subsequent employment, while

Table 13. **Participants in ALMP programmes**

	1998	1999	2000	2001	2002
FAS training programmes	12 108	12 959	12 301	11 158	14 167
Community employment	40 000	38 927	36 131	33 571	24 991
Back to work allowance	14 520	18 483	19 943	15 973	13 510
Back to work enterprise allowance	9 733	19 117	19 148	15 973	13 510
Vocational training opportunities scheme	4 630	5 169	5 298	5 544	5 699
Tourism training	11 545	10 915	10 946	12 022	11 795
Total	92 536	100 401	98 469	94 241	83 672
Reference:					
Number of unemployed	106 100	88 700	68 800	79 500	84 100

Source: FAS.

skills training and employment subsidies have some positive impacts (O'Connell, 2002). A special unit of the Department of Finance, which evaluated the employment and human resource development programmes under the National Development Plan, also concluded that employment support schemes are characterised by large deadweight losses and should be curtailed. Among them, the *Community Employment Scheme* (CES) is not only the largest direct employment scheme but also a single biggest component of the ALMP, which provided some 25 000 jobs in 2002. Although the participants have received training in addition to work experience, their employability has tended to remain weak as they are the most difficult cases given their poor educational and social background.[75] Consequently, the CES has become, in a way, a source of regular employment. The government reduced the size of this scheme from 33 500 in 2001 to 25 000 in 2002. But this has been achieved partly through transferring CE funds to grants for school ancillary service so as to allow schools to keep employing temporary workers who used to be financed directly by CE funds. Since the number of long-term unemployed fell much more rapidly than did those on the CES, a more substantial downsizing would be required through tightening eligibility.[76]

On the other hand, *Back to Work Allowance Scheme* and another similar scheme, *Back to Work Enterprise Allowance*, provide income support for long-term unemployed claimants to return to work or to enter self-employment. These schemes, under which 27 000 people receive income supports, are intended to subsidise jobs in the market place. It has been reported that they have proved successful in enabling transition from unemployment to work. An important issue, however, is how to contain the deadweight cost through a programme design. Indeed, the government tightened the eligibility for these schemes by raising the required period of being unemployed from 12 to 15 months. This change resulted in a decline in the number of recipients of the subsidies from 39 000 in 2000 to 32 000 in 2001 and to 27 000 in 2002.

Recently, under the *National Employment Action Plan* (NEAP) the government has placed more emphasis on preventing people from becoming long-term unemployed. In that scheme, the Department of Social, Community and Family Affairs refers the unemployed to FAS for an interview if they remain jobless for more than a certain length of time. The scheme, introduced in 1998, covered all those under 25 years of age and unemployed for more than six months. An experiment carried out in Kilkenny and Ballyfermot to expand this type of intervention to cover all the unemployed of over 6 months suggests that such incremental intervention might be responsible for a more rapid decline in unemployment in those regions than nationally.[77] Subsequently, the process has been expanded so that, in addition to the original group, all unemployed people between the ages of 25 to 54 are called in for an interview if they pass the nine-month threshold. Given the inefficiency existing in the current ALMP schemes, such a shift towards preventive measures goes in the right direction.

Immigration development

Although the inflow of immigrants has been an important source of growth in labour force in recent years, the government begins to move towards tightening work permits as it faced some rise in unemployment rate, while experiencing a sharp rise in applicants for work permits. The system of work permit allows employers to recruit workers from non-European Economic countries to fill their vacancies registered at FAS. However, the past issuance of work permits resulted in supporting the inflow of unskilled labour as many of those who were recruited under this scheme work in such areas as hotel, tourism and catering (27 per cent of work permit personnel), agriculture services (16 per cent), while only a limited number of them are engaged in medical and nursing care and other professional jobs.[78] Consequently, 70 per cent of work permit personnel receive less than € 350 per week, which is significantly less than the average earnings.[79] Since the strong growth of the economy in the past several years increased the demand of employers for cheaper non-EEA workers, the issued work permits increased sharply from 6 000 in 1999 to 36 000 in 2001. Against this background, the government has tightened the conditions on the application for work permit since January 2002 so that applications can be accepted only after employers make a real effort to find EEA nationals to fill their vacancies. On the other hand, a number of surveys suggest the necessity to rely on immigration to alleviate labour shortage for professionals and skilled manual workers. As a result, migration policy has begun to place more emphasis on attracting skilled migrants, rather than simply preventing the inflow of unskilled workers. But the shortage of housing and high living costs, both of which are the most serious constraints on the inflow of skilled workers, need to be tackled.

Some aspects of sustainable development

There is growing concern that long-run sustainable development may be compromised unless countries take measures to achieve balance between economic, environmental and social outcomes. This section looks at three issues of environmentally sustainable development that are of particular importance for Ireland. In each case, indicators are presented to measure the progress and the evolution of potential problems, and an assessment is made of government policies that affect the issue. The section also considers whether institutional arrangements are in place to integrate policymaking across the different elements of sustainable development (see Box 11). The section looks at the policies that aim at controlling emissions of greenhouse gases, reducing water pollution and dealing with waste.

Box 11. Policy integration across sustainable development areas[1]

The co-ordination of policies across sustainable development areas is still being developed in Ireland. The National Sustainable Development Strategy adopted in 1997 focused mainly on environmental goals but marked the first systematic attempt to integrate their pursuit into sectoral economic policies. In conjunction with the transposition of an EU directive of 1997 that mandates environmental impact assessments (EIAs) of large publicly funded projects, this gave a large role to EIAs in the formulation of the National Development Plan for 2000-2006. These assessments have not, however, included any monetary valuation of environmental outcomes, so failing to integrate the economic and environmental dimensions of sustainable development. As to institutional arrangements regarding government and civil society, the implementation of the 1997 Sustainable Development Strategy has led to the establishment of numerous bodies aiming at a better co-ordination and consultation.

On the other hand, there is a lack of integration between environmental and social objectives. The recent update on the sustainable development strategy makes an attempt to put more emphasis on social goals (DELG, 2002). Objectives of social policy are listed side-by-side with environmental goals but can hardly be regarded as integrated in a comprehensive strategy. The concomitant decision to increase the use of massively subsidised and environmentally harmful peat is particularly telling in this regard (see section on climate change below).

Beside institutional arrangements, cost-benefit analysis (CBA) is an helpful tool to arbitrate the trade-offs among sometimes conflicting objectives as they arise in the pursuit of sustainable development. Its use remains limited to particular cases as there is no legal requirement for the government to conduct CBA prior to making decisions, in contrast with the mandate to estimate costs to the budget and to conduct an EIA. A comprehensive CBA was undertaken in the context of the preparation of the Climate Change Strategy (ERM, 1998) and proved useful though its conclusions were ignored as far as peat was concerned. In the area of water pollution, there is no doubt that a CBA of the decision to withdraw water charges in 1997 would have usefully informed Irish citizens and taxpayers.

1. The sections in this report dealing with climate change, water pollution and waste are inputs into the Organisation's follow up on Sustainable Development as mandated by the Ministerial Council decision in May 2001.

Climate change

Main issues

Within the EU burden-sharing agreement that distributes the overall EU objective of reducing total GHG emissions by 8 per cent from their 1990 level by the period 2008-2012, Ireland negotiated a target that allows its emissions to rise to 13 per cent above their 1990 level. The main issue for Ireland is to comply with its European commitment without imposing an excessive burden on the economy.

Performance

The level of GHG emissions per unit of GDP has been reduced in Ireland over the 1990s at a much more rapid rate than the OECD average (Table 14). This is largely because economic expansion occurred primarily in relatively low-emitting sectors such as information technology and pharmaceuticals and resulted in a marked improvement in CO_2 emission efficiency in manufacturing (Table 15). In contrast, there was limited improvement in emission intensity in the

Table 14. **Main indicators: climate change**

Indicators of greenhouse gas (GHG) emission intensity, grammes of CO_2 equivalent per $PPP of GDP, in 1995 prices

	Total GHG emissions	CO_2 emissions, electricity	CO_2 emissions, transport	Other GHG emissions	Total GHG emissions	CO_2 emissions, electricity	CO_2 emissions, transport	Other GHG emissions
	Level, 1999				Average annual percentage change 1990-1999			
Australia	1 053	370	155	528	–2.07	–0.21	–1.93	–3.24
Austria	419	72	91	256	–1.87	–2.75	–0.52	–2.06
Belgium	617	97	101	419	–1.36	–2.12	0.16	–1.52
Canada	893	151	193	549	–0.98	–0.12	–0.36	–1.41
Czech Republic	1 058	457	88	513	–3.05	2.55	5.53	–6.93
Denmark	549	194	94	261	–1.64	–1.43	–1.49	–1.85
Finland	652	181	105	366	–1.88	–0.02	–1.29	–2.83
France	416	32	103	280	–1.69	–2.04	0.16	–2.26
Germany	536	169	96	271	–4.00	–3.86	–0.57	–5.05
Greece	813	275	130	408	–0.24	0.07	0.74	–0.73
Hungary	786	250	84	453	–2.33	1.44	0.38	–3.74
Iceland	395	4	88	303	–1.28	0.00	–2.31	0.81
Ireland	**694**	**165**	**103**	**426**	**–4.27**	**–2.41**	**0.79**	**–5.75**
Italy	439	105	92	242	–1.05	–0.82	0.37	–1.64
Japan	432	130	82	221	–0.30	–0.03	1.24	–0.99
Luxembourg	344	6	242	97	–11.46	–30.20	–0.45	–18.81
Netherlands	573	138	82	352	–2.38	–1.03	–0.94	–3.15
New Zealand	1 096	92	175	828	–2.28	4.58	0.65	–3.32
Norway	487	4	113	369	–2.54	1.31	–1.53	–2.87
Poland	1 195	481	90	624	–4.96	–6.63	0.50	–4.12
Portugal	540	149	106	285	0.41	2.58	3.37	–1.39
Slovakia	957	200	76	680	–4.47	–1.21	3.13	–5.78
Spain	537	127	130	280	0.41	1.12	1.28	–0.26
Sweden	358	41	112	204	–1.55	0.07	–0.65	–2.30
Switzerland	276	3	79	195	–0.62	–1.96	–0.28	–0.73
United Kingdom	526	132	108	287	–3.66	–5.30	–1.38	–3.61
United States	792	278	196	318	–1.89	–0.60	–1.18	–3.28
OECD total	649	196	140	312	–1.80	–0.98	–0.38	–2.83
EU	506	120	103	283	–2.36	–2.60	–0.16	–2.95

Source: Greenhouse gas emissions: national submissions to the UNFCCC and national publications. Carbon dioxide emissions for electricity and transport: IEA (2001). GDP: OECD, SNA database.

Table 15. GHG emissions and sectoral indicators

	Total GHG emissions		CO_2 emissions per Kwh electricity	Manufacturing CO_2 emissions per unit of industrial production	Residential CO_2 emissions per unit of private consumption	Road transport CO_2 emissions per vehicle	Electricity use per unit of GDP	Industrial output per unit of GDP
	Level million tonnes CO_2 equivalent 1999	Annual average percentage change						
		1990-1999[1,2]				1990-1998	1990-1999	
Australia	489	1.6	0.4	–0.5	–2.0	–1.7	–0.6	–1.9
Austria	80	0.3	–2.5	–3.1	–4.6	–1.8	–0.2	1.1
Belgium	151	0.6	–2.0	–1.0	–1.3	0.0	–0.1	–0.3
Canada	699	1.6	0.4	–3.1	–3.4	1.4	–0.6	1.0
Czech Republic	138	–3.4	1.9	–12.6	–11.4	–1.4	0.6	1.7
Denmark	73	0.6	–3.7	–3.6	–5.5	0.5	2.4	0.8
Finland	76	–0.1	–1.0	–5.4	–7.7	–0.6	1.0	2.9
France	549	–0.1	–2.8	–1.5	–1.2	0.1	0.8	–0.2
Germany	994	–2.3	–2.2	–2.7	–5.0	–2.6	–1.7	–0.9
Greece	124	1.9	–1.7	–1.6	8.0	–1.1	1.8	–1.4
Hungary	84	–2.0	–1.2	–13.5	10.0	–2.0	2.7	6.2
Iceland	3	1.1	..	..	–8.5	–1.6	2.9	..
Ireland	**65**	**2.2**	**–0.6**	**–11.2**	**–5.6**	**3.5**	**–1.8**	**5.6**
Italy	540	0.4	–1.6	–1.8	0.4	0.4	0.8	–0.4
Japan	1 328	1.0	–1.1	0.7	–2.3	0.1	1.1	–1.9
Luxembourg	6	–6.4	–21.5	–13.8	–1.2	1.0	–11.1	–3.3
Netherlands	218	0.4	–0.3	–2.4	–4.1	–0.2	–0.7	–0.8
New Zealand	76	0.5	5.6	0.3	–3.4	–0.6	–0.9	–1.0
Norway	56	0.9	4.8	–2.0	–7.8	0.9	–3.4	–1.5
Poland	400	–1.5	–3.7	–6.3	15.6	–1.7	–3.0	3.8
Portugal	86	3.1	0.6	1.2	1.9	–0.4	2.0	–1.2
Slovakia	53	–3.6	–2.0	–6.3	–0.4	0.6	0.9	–2.4
Spain	371	2.9	0.1	–1.5	1.9	–0.2	1.0	–0.4
Sweden	71	0.0	1.0	–4.0	–4.1	0.4	–0.9	1.5
Switzerland	53	0.0	–3.8	0.1	–2.5	–0.7	1.9	1.0

Table 15. **GHG emissions and sectoral indicators** (*cont.*)

	Total GHG emissions		CO_2 emissions per Kwh electricity	Manufacturing CO_2 emissions per unit of industrial production	Residential CO_2 emissions per unit of private consumption	Road transport CO_2 emissions per vehicle	Electricity use per unit of GDP	Industrial output per unit of GDP
	Level million tonnes CO_2 equivalent 1999	Annual average percentage change						
		1990-1999[1,2]				1990-1998	1990-1999	
United Kingdom	647	–1.5	–4.7	–1.7	–0.7	–0.2	–0.7	–1.6
United States	6 830	1.2	0.2	–5.3	–2.3	1.1	0.8	1.2
Total of above OECD countries	14 257	0.5	–0.7	–3.1	–1.6	0.1	–0.3	0.1
OECD excluding US	**7 428**	**0.0**	**–1.8**	**–2.0**	**–1.1**	**–0.6**	**0.0**	**–0.6**
EU countries	4 048	–0.4	–2.4	–2.2	–2.0	–0.6	–0.2	–0.5

1. 1995-1999 for Czech Republic; 1991-1999 for Germany; 1992-1999 for Hungary and Slovakia; no data for Iceland.
2. 1991-1998 for Czech Republic; 1995-1999 for Slovakia.

Source: GHG National submissions to UNFCCC, national sources and UNFCCC; carbon dioxide data, IEA; industrial production, private consumption, OECD.

electricity sector due to the cost of pipeline connections to the United Kingdom and limitations on the capacity of existing infrastructures. Emissions, however, rose by 24 per cent between 1990 and 2000. Agriculture is responsible for over a quarter of emissions, because of nitrous oxide and methane from fertiliser and livestock, respectively. Overall, the reduction in the ratio of emissions to GDP was outweighed by rapid economic growth (7¼ per cent against 2¾ per cent in the area as a whole) and Ireland's total GHG emissions rose during the 1990s at the third highest rate in the OECD area (Table 15). With the policies in place by 2000, official estimates suggested that emissions were set to rise to 37 per cent above their 1990 level by 2010.

Policies

In November 2000, the government published a new National Climate Change Strategy with the objective of bringing emissions into line with the 2008-12 target. The Strategy establishes indicative quantitative abatement targets for broad economic sectors, with electricity generation accounting for the largest cuts. It specified in broad terms the kind of instruments that would be used to attain the targets in each sector, including carbon tax, emission trading, command-and-control regulations and voluntary agreements. Many of the key measures to implement the Strategy have yet to be introduced and some continue to be postponed. For example, the government announced in its 2003 budget that it planned to introduce a carbon tax from the end of 2004. With permit trading starting at the EU level, the tax could serve to capture part of the value of grandfathered permits.

According to government estimates, three-quarters of the emission reduction in the electricity sector is to come about through switching from coal to natural gas, with the expanded use of renewable energy, notably wind power, contributing much of the remaining planned cuts. If electricity producers are to be induced to switch from coal to gas on commercial grounds, this would require either relatively high taxes on carbon or high permit prices (Table 16) – in the absence of any compensation for air pollution externalities – due to the heavy transport costs for gas in Ireland. Some oil plants have been replaced by gas ones, as the government allocated transport rights for this use. New pipelines will shortly be opened. However, the government also committed itself to not taxing inputs into the electricity sector but rather to taxing its output. The government acknowledged that the former would be more efficient but felt that such a tax would have a disproportionate impact on the domestic production of peat and so would affect the security of energy supply. Consequently, there is some doubt about whether fuel switching will start until quota trading is introduced in the EU. The expansion of wind power is part of the government's commitment to meeting its target for renewable energy as set by the EU. In order to meet this objective,

Table 16. **Influence of a carbon tax on the costs of power generation**

Technology	€ per tonne of carbon equivalent		
	0	20	73
Coal – existing plant	0.0263	0.0307	0.0425
Coal plus flue gas desulphurisation	0.0298[1]	0.0344[1]	0.0465
Oil – existing plant	0.0525	0.0566	0.0674
Gas – existing plant	0.0537	0.0565	0.0638
Gas – new combined cycle gas turbine	0.0424	0.0443	0.0494
Gas – new open cycle gas turbine	0.0633	0.0664	0.0745
Peat – existing	0.0837	0.0926	0.1163
Peat – new	0.0493	0.0554	0.0718
Hydro	0.0281	0.0281	0.0281
Wind – new	0.0415	0.0415	0.0415[1]
Wind and gas open cycle gas turbine	0.0524	0.0539	0.0580

1. Least cost.
Source: Bergin *et al.* (2002) and OECD Secretariat computations.

the government obligated electricity companies to offer 15-year fixed price contracts for wind power and then auctioned these contracts. Although the auction method ensures that wind power is expanded at least cost, the premium demanded over average electricity prices was 1.27 eurocents (36 per cent of the average wholesale price of electricity[80]). If the renewable electricity replaces coal-based generating plants then the premium could be justified by reduced air pollution costs alone. On the other hand, if new pipelines lower the price of gas, so making it the fuel of choice for new plants, then externalities, including those from air pollution, would only outweigh the renewable premium if carbon prices were above current projections of EU permit prices. The cost of the renewable premium will be passed to the consumer as an additional levy.[81]

In addition, the Climate Change Strategy calls for cuts in emissions in a range of sectors, including some where abatement costs are estimated to be much higher than for renewable energy (Table 17): in *industry*, voluntary agreements form the backbone of the programme, especially for the cement, fertiliser and semi-conductor industries. In other industries the government suggests agreements may cost up to € 931 per tonne of carbon. In *agriculture*, research will be undertaken to develop feeding regimes that reduce methane emission from livestock. Farmers receiving payments under the CAP rural development plan and other investment schemes will be required to implement best management practices for fertiliser. In the *transport sector*, the major national emission saving action promised in the Strategy will be to raise transport fuel taxation. Such an increase would be line with air pollution externalities (see below) and also reflect the higher carbon content of diesel fuel. The vehicle registration tax will be progressively raised on larger cars.

Table 17. **Sectoral abatement costs under the Climate Strategy *versus* imports of permits**

	GHG emissions saved per year	Yearly cost	Yearly unit cost
	Million tons of carbon equivalent	€ million	€ per ton of carbon equivalent
Energy supply	1.54	44	29
Transport	0.73	102	139
Buildings	0.25	37	150
Industry	0.55	254[1]	466
Agriculture	0.66	127	193
Total of above domestic actions	3.72	564	
Waste	0.45	{ Costs attributed to waste and forestry policies	
Sinks	0.21		
Memorandum item:			
Buying permits abroad	3.72	74	20[2]

1. This is a Secretariat estimate based on the original marginal cost of € 931 per tonne of carbon (= Ir200/tonne of CO_2) reported in the strategy. A quadratic cost curve has been fixed to reflect the presence of low-cost options that are then supplemented by increasingly costlier actions, up to € 931 per tonne of carbon.
2. Upper estimate reported in IEA (2002).

Source: Secretariat computation on the basis of values reported in the *National Climate Change Strategy.*

A notable absence from the Climate Change Strategy was any action to reduce the use of peat in power generation. This fuel is even more carbon-intensive than coal and accounts for 8 per cent of total electricity generation. A new plant burning the fuel came on line in December 2000, aided by capital subsidies paid from the general budget and the EU Economic Infrastructure Operational Programme. Two further plants are to come into operation in 2004 and in 2005, replacing plants that have reached the end of their life. As to the existing plants, their excessive operating costs need subsidies that constitute the bulk (85 per cent) of the extra tax (€ 46 million) charged on domestic electricity sales. (CER, 2002). Even when putting a zero price on CO_2 emissions, electricity generated by modern peat plants still cost more than that produced by coal, gas and wind (Table 17). Continued use of peat deprives Ireland of a negative cost option for lowering emissions and hence raises compliance costs in the rest of the economy.

Conclusions

The National Climate Change Strategy embodies a promising approach in that it proposes the use of economic instruments such as carbon taxation and permit trading. It is therefore unfortunate that the Strategy ruled out the use of carbon taxation on fuel inputs in the electricity sector. More generally the government feels that such taxation would endanger the use of peat as a fuel. However, the introduction of the EU permit trading scheme will obviate the need to tax inputs in the electricity sector. Subsidies to the peat industry should not be increased when carbon permit trading is introduced. Intrinsically inefficient negotiated agreements with industry would be usefully superseded by the trading scheme. As to transport, the government should build on its recent decision to raise diesel excise taxes and aim to equalise taxes on gasoline and diesel with their respective externalities.

Reducing water pollution

Main issues

A good quality supply of surface and ground water helps the provision of clean drinking water, an essential commodity. Unpolluted rivers also provide a base for many recreational and economic activities, being crucial to the appeal of the countryside for tourists. With their quality deteriorating recently, Ireland's Sustainable Development strategy has identified eutrophication as "the most serious environmental problem" (DELG, 2002). EU directives aim at preventing any deterioration of water quality from current levels by 2015 and to managing water by river basin. The main challenge is to achieve this goal while keeping costs in check.

Performance

Ireland's surface waters are generally in very good condition, with 70 per cent of watercourses' length classified as unpolluted. However, 85 per cent of watercourses length were unpolluted three decades ago (OECD, 2000) and the long-lasting trend decline in water quality was reversed only very recently (Figure 15), thanks to the increase in the share of the population connected to primary or secondary sewage treatment facilities. Twenty years ago nitrate concentrations were close to the European average but, in the most recent three years for which data is available, have risen to some 25 per cent above the average European level (Table 18) and are particularly high levels in the south east. Phosphorus concentrations are also building up (EPA, 2002b). In both cases, farming accounts for three-quarters of total pollution loads.[82] The quality of groundwater is also worrisome with 38 per cent of sampled wells showing contamination by *e.coli* bacteria and 20 per cent of samples presenting excessive concentrations of nitrates. At least 9 per cent of the Irish state should be designated as a nitrate vulnerable zone (European Commission, 2002).

Policies

The main focus of water policy is on water services. Substantial investments have been made during the 1990s both to secure the supply of safe drinking water and to treat waste water (Figure 16). Non-domestic demand for water will start to be restrained by price in 2006 with the introduction of meters, but

Figure 15. **Quality of surface water in Ireland**

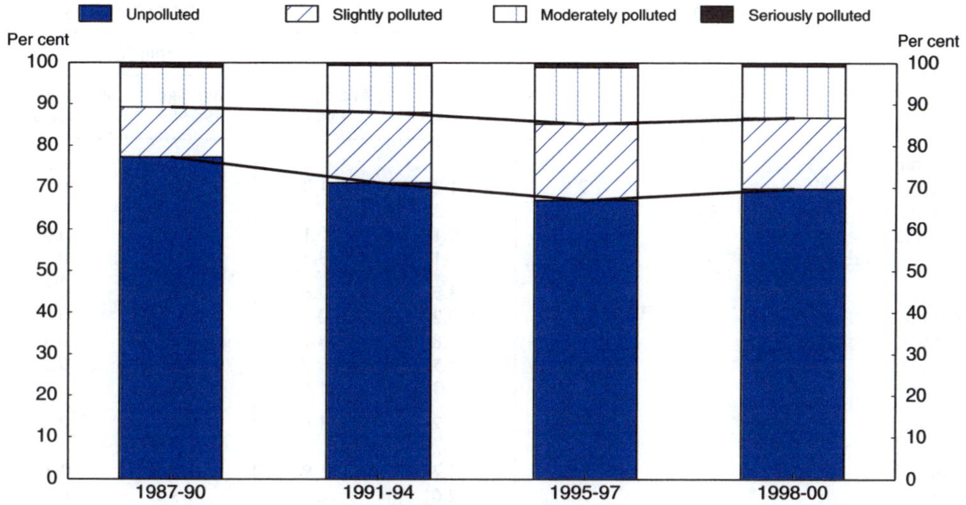

Source: EPA, 2002.

household water distribution and treatment will continue to be financed from taxation. This could lead to continued increases in water usage outrunning treatment capacity and also requiring excessive and economically inefficient use of water purification services. Indeed, annual investments in water services are set to rise to the equivalent of 1.1 per cent of GDP in the 2002-2004 period, and operating costs are expected to more than double between 2001 and 2008. The financial incentives governing the provision of water services are unlikely to keep costs in check: the local authorities commission investment and operate facilities, but all capital costs and most current expenditure are financed by the central government.

Water policy has placed less emphasis on agriculture although this sector is the chief cause of eutrophication (EPA, 2002). Agricultural activities were for long exempt from any measures aiming at reducing water pollution, as local authorities chose not to exercise their power to regulate farmers. As a result, central government has taken a greater role in recent years and introduced a mix of regulations and subsidies. Integrated pollution licensing, introduced for industry in 1994, has been expanded since 1996 to big livestock units, mainly poultry and pig farms.

The main policy instrument for reducing diffuse emissions of nitrates has been the rural environment protection scheme (REPS) which offers subsidies, of a maximum € 5 000 per farm and per annum, to farmers who sign a code of good practice. In addition, direct support payments under the common agricultural

Table 18. **Performance indicators: water pollution**
Selected rivers

	Biochemical oxygen demand		Nitrates		Total phosphorus	
	mg O2/litre		mg N/litre		mg P/litre	
	Average 1980-85	Average last 3 years	Average 1980-85	Average last 3 years	Average 1980-85	Average last 3 years
Australia	..	..	..	..	..	..
Austria	2.2	2.2	1.2	1.3	0.2	0.1
Belgium	6.6	..	3.8	..	0.7	..
Canada	..	..	0.1	0.1	0.1	0.0
Czech Republic	8.5	4.6	5.1	3.5	..	0.3
Denmark	3.9	2.0	3.5	2.6	0.3	0.1
Finland	..	..	0.2	0.3	0.0	0.0
France	5.2	3.2	2.8	3.1	0.4	0.4
Germany	3.6	2.4	3.5	3.3	0.5	0.2
Greece	..	..	1.3	1.5	0.4	0.4
Hungary	4.4	2.9	2.2	1.6	0.4	0.3
Iceland	..	..	..	..	..	..
Ireland	**1.7**	**1.8**	**2.2**	**2.9**	**0.1**	**0.1**
Italy	..	..	2.0	2.1	0.3	0.2
Japan	2.3	1.4	..	..	..	..
Korea	..	2.8	..	2.6	..	0.1
Luxembourg	3.8	2.7	4.1	4.1	0.6	0.4
Mexico	3.7	15.9	1.9	0.6	..	0.1
Netherlands	2.8	3.1	4.4	3.3	0.5	0.2
New Zealand	..	..	..	..	..	..
Norway	..	..	0.3	0.3	0.0	0.0
Poland	5.0	4.3	1.8	1.9	0.3	0.3
Portugal	..	..	..	..	..	..
Slovak Republic	5.1	3.3	2.0	2.2	0.1	0.2
Spain	4.7	3.6	1.7	3.1	0.6	0.2
Sweden	..	..	0.4	0.5	0.0	0.1
Switzerland	..	..	1.5	1.5	0.1	0.1
Turkey	2.1	2.7	1.3	1.0	0.3	0.2
United Kingdom	3.4	2.9	4.6	5.2	0.8	0.9
United States	1.8	1.6	1.1	..	0.2	0.1

Source: OECD.

policy (CAP), that amount to one quarter of farm revenue, have also been made conditional upon good farming practice. Besides, these incentives do influence the most polluting farms as they would not gain from joining REPS and, moreover, benefit primarily from CAP price support mechanisms rather than direct payments which cannot easily be made conditional. Nonetheless, 93 per cent of the 140 000 farms adhere to the code of good practice.

Figure 16. **Financial costs of water pollution.**

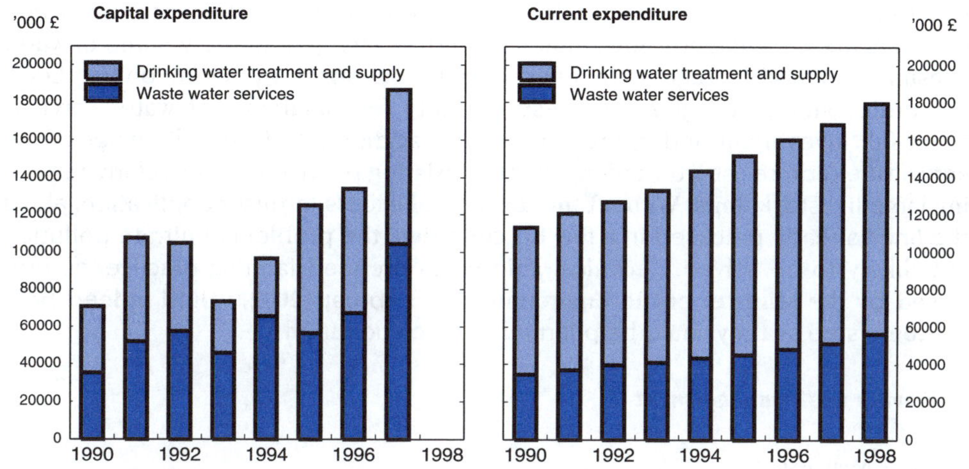

Source: Scott *et al.*, 2001.

At the beginning of 2002, the government proposed to designate the whole territory as an nitrate vulnerable zone under the EU Council Nitrate Directive. This approach was adopted in preference to an approach based on zones because it was felt that such a policy would result in discrimination between farmers engaged in similar activities but outside vulnerable zones. When legislation is passed limits will apply to the quantity of livestock manure that can be spread on farmland. Intensive livestock operations with inadequate land to service their operations will have to transport their slurry to farms that have a deficit. Taking a national approach will also mean all farmers will be eligible for subsidies of up to 55 per cent of the cost of waste stockage facilities, a policy that has been very expensive in some other European countries, In addition, farmers will have to comply with a code of good farming practices in line with the code that already applies to farmers who benefit from REPS payments. Careful monitoring of nitrate levels in water, especially in the areas that had been identified as being polluted, or susceptible to pollution. A complement to the regulatory approach might be to apply a tax on the over-application of nutrients (including animal manure from intensive livestock farms) though establishing the economically justifiable tax rate might be difficult. Keeping precise records of nutrient balances would be complicated but, as in Denmark and the Netherlands, should be possible in areas where excess nutrient discharge is a problem.

Conclusions

Preserving Ireland's largely clean surface waters and restoring its too often polluted underground water without inflicting escalating costs on the economy requires putting an end to a situation where, apart from industry, water users and polluters are not charged. Households should be charged for the volume of water consumed. Possible regressive effects could be offset by social policy. Local authorities should be given the responsibility for ensuring that water services cover full investment and operating costs. In addition, reducing discharges from agriculture requires stricter enforcement of existing provisions, particularly regarding large livestock units. Without the taxation of excess fertiliser application, along the lines already practised in a few EU countries, the problem of nitrate pollution is unlikely to be solved. Technical guidelines on good farming practice, as proposed by the Minister of the Environment in February 2002, would indeed be a welcome step as they could help farmers reduce pollution.

Improving waste management

Main issues

If mishandled, the disposal of waste can cause long-lasting damage to ecosystems and to human health, involving negative externalities such as leakage to aquifers and to surface waters from landfills. With waste production on the rise, Ireland is facing a shortage of capacity in landfills. Hence the need to implement cost-effective long-term solutions while complying with stringent EU directives.

Performance

The per capita amount of municipal waste generation is among the highest in Europe. Over the long term the ratio of household waste consumption has risen significantly, although more recently these trends appear to have reversed due to the introduction of new recycling schemes. In comparison with other European countries, only a limited share of municipal waste is recycled (Table 19). All other waste is landfilled since there are no municipal waste incinerators. The remaining municipal landfill capacity of about 10 million tonnes would accommodate less than five years of municipal and construction waste production (EPA, 2002).

Policies

The cost of landfilling has risen more than eightfold since the mid-1990s, jumping from € 5-12 per tonne in 1996 to € 43-78 in 2000 (Eunomia, 2002). This partly reflects the fact that EU regulations and an increased awareness of environmental issues have put a strong pressure on a deficient infrastructure, as only

Table 19. **Performance indicators: waste**

	Municipal waste					
	Level	Relative to private consumption	Annual growth		Recycling	Composting
	Kg per capita, latest available year[1]	Grammes per US$, 1995 PPPs	Period	Per cent	Per cent of total, latest available year[1]	
Australia	..	..	–	..	..	..
Austria	548	45.5	1990-1999	3.7	24	40
Belgium	534	47.0	1990-1999	3.0	37	15
Canada	..	..	–	..	..	..
Czech Republic	334	54.2	1990-2000	..	..	..
Denmark	626	57.4	1994-1999	3.5	25	14
Finland	464	49.0	1990-1999	–2.8	..	..
France	524	46.4	1993-1999	1.7	10	8
Germany	549	46.0	1991-1998	–1.5	41	..
Greece	371	42.7	1990-1997	3.8	8	1
Hungary	444	85.7	1990-2000	–1.9	0	0
Iceland	718	52.7	1992-2000	2.8	9	2
Ireland	615	49.5	1995-2000	8.2	8	1
Italy	497	40.1	1990-1999	4.0	7	10
Japan	406	34.6	1990-1999	0.2	9	..
Korea	364	50.3	1990-2000	–5.8	41	..
Luxembourg	643	38.7	1991-1999	3.1	0	12
Mexico	315	63.5	1991-1000	4.3	2	0
Netherlands	613	53.3	1991-1000	2.9	23	24
New Zealand	..	..	–	..	..	..
Norway	617	51.2	1992-2000	2.7	22	9
Poland	316	64.0	1990-2000	1.0	0	2
Portugal	437	50.7	1992-1999	4.2	4	5
Slovakia	316	58.2	1992-2000	..	2	5
Spain	464	48.0	1990-1999	4.3	5	18
Sweden	452	47.5	1990-1998	2.8	25	8
Switzerland	655	41.8	1990-1000	1.4	32	14
Turkey	385	101.4	1989-1998	..	0	1
United Kingdom	558	44.8	1990-1999	2.3	9	2
United States	764	35.7	1990-1999	1.3	22	6
OECD average	501	42.3		1.3	17	7
EU average	526	45.6		1.9	18	10

1. 2000 for Ireland.
Source: OECD, Eurostat. For Spain: national submissions.

40 per cent of the landfills licensed for municipal waste had collection systems for the liquids that leak from landfills in 1994 (COWI, 2002). This has led to closures of numerous small and poorly-managed landfills and to massive investment in others, with local authorities passing some of the cost to households and businesses.

Strong public opposition to new landfills and the lack of a regional waste management framework have hindered the adjustment in landfill capacity although some expansion has been taking place. In this context, most local authorities have given overriding priority to municipal refuse over industrial and construction waste in landfills in order to avoid an immediate shortage of capacity. There has also been opposition to incinerators, but local authorities are now planning to open three facilities by 2005, helped by central government grants. As the legally available capacity is most likely to be insufficient for current estimated flows of construction waste, some illegal dumping may occur, especially as enforcement and penalties seem too weak to make illegal operations uneconomic (Peter Bacon and Associates, 2002).

In this situation, waste policy has brought recycling and waste prevention into focus. In the area of packaging materials, an EU directive required 25 per cent recovery by 2001. This target has been met by means of a producer responsibility scheme in which producers of packaged goods pay a contribution to Repak. This company subsidises local authorities to separate household waste streams and guarantees an economic return to contractors that recover or recycle waste from all sectors of the economy. In 2001, Repak spent € 55 per tonne of recycled packaging material, the second lowest compliance cost in Europe. If major efforts are made to increase recycling, marginal costs are likely to rise, Especially as market size limits the extent of local reprocessing capacity (Eunomia, 2002), so forcing export of both raw and processed waste with resulting increases in transport costs. It would then be necessary to balance the increased cost of recycling against the cost of other forms of waste disposal such as adequately regulated landfills and incineration. In order to reduce litter, the government introduced a Plastic Shopping Bag Levy in March 2002. According to first estimates, this € 0.15 tax on every plastic bag has brought down the number of bags used to about 5 per cent of previous consumption, *i.e.* 95 per cent reduction.

The government has also introduced a landfill levy which collects € 15 per tonne for the Environmental Fund. The landfill levy, which is approximately equal to estimated externalities from old sites, is intended to discourage landfill and to promote both reduction at the source and recycling. For this to work, this extra cost has to be felt by those that produce waste. In this regard, the landfill levy seems well suited for industrial and construction waste. Households currently have no incentive to reduce their production of waste since the charges are levied on a flat-rate basis. The government plans universal weight charging by 2005. Although cost recovery has improved in recent years with waste charges being levied everywhere in Ireland since the beginning of 2002, the charges only cover 30 per cent of outlays on municipal waste. Progressively these charges will be moved to a volume or weight based system that should become the norm by 2005. Such a system should give households an incentive to reduce waste generation and increase participation in segregated waste collection that allows recycling.

Conclusions

Waste policy has moved in the direction of using economic instruments to achieve mandated targets. A landfill tax has been introduced, volume-based waste charging will be introduced and packaging waste is being recycled through a producer levy that is among the lowest in Europe. At the same time, the government has introduced regulations to ensure that all new landfill sites employ state-of-the art environmental protection technology. For the future, care has to be taken to ensure that economic instruments are set at values that reflect externalities and are consistent across different methods of waste disposal, including recycling. In particular, the highly competitive level of the fees charged by the recycling organisation needs to be safeguarded. Short-term landfill and recycling capacity problems need to be overcome by means of a co-ordinated approach at the regional level.

Notes

1. For 2002, a decline in profits of Irish companies operating abroad was an additional factor.
2. Congestion, as measured by the weighted average of the time taken to travel fourteen radial routes and two major orbital routes around the Dublin city centre at peak times, has increased by nearly 25 per cent between 1999 and 2002. It is very likely that the congestion problem worsened a lot more than this if compared with the situation say in 1995, but no study was carried out prior to 1999. Alternatively, one can look at the comparison of actual speed with "free-flow speed". According to the Dublin transport office the average "free-flow speed" (where traffic is flowing freely) is 22 to 24 kilometres per hour. The data indicates that the majority of routes were well below this level even in 1999. The (simple) average in 1999 was 18 km/h and further deteriorated to 16 km/h in 2002. The congestion problem is likely to impact adversely on staff costs, the willingness of some of the labour force to travel into the city centre, and firms' motivation to set up business within the capital.
3. The volume of manufacturing output is being driven by a small number of sectors. Evidence from the Census of Industrial Production suggests that it is these modern sectors of the economy that dominate the manufacturing sector. Chemicals accounts for 35 per cent of net output, food products for 14.4 per cent, and optical and electrical equipment for 25 per cent of which 18 per cent is for ICT. Given the extent to which the chemical sector dominates output it is interesting to note that the sector accounts for just 9 per cent of employment. Annual growth in the chemicals sector consistently outperformed total manufacturing in the late 1990s. Provisional figures for 2002 show that the volume of output in the chemicals, chemical products and man-made fibres sector rose by 24 per cent compared with 8 per cent growth for total manufacturing. The narrow base of current buoyancy in industrial activity is mirrored in the export figures. The detailed breakdown of the value of exports by sector indicates that the main sector to show value growth was chemicals and related products.
4. The indigenous, more employment-intensive, industries with the greater exposure to non-euro area trade would be particularly vulnerable to sustained euro appreciation.
5. The budget assumptions behind the OECD forecasts are in line with the government's Stability Programme Update of December 2002.
6. One example of this is a company like Pfizer who moved to Ireland as a manufacturing plant but who have announced a move to put in a treasury arm into the Dublin IFSC given the demonstration effect of the success of other firms in the financial sector. Another example of existing clients moving up the value chain is Apple in Cork. It used to be a large scale manufacturing plant but is now the European Headquarters for Apple. It has the European (multi-lingual) customer relations centre and technical support, on-line electronic sales, and a range of important functions including Treasury,

Order Management, Logistics, and Data Centre. The result is that today 70 per cent of Apple's Irish workforce are in high value services. All these functions have been integrated into one highly cost effective model adding value to Apple Inc. and increasing its embeddedness in Ireland.

7. Much of the recent literature on the effects of infrastructure on growth has focused on the estimation of the rate of return to infrastructure, which is inferred from the output elasticity of infrastructure. For Ireland only two published studies exist, with one finding an output elasticity with respect to infrastructure that is not statistically significantly different from zero, implying that infrastructure adds nothing to output, while the other finds unrealistically high output elasticities. Given the infrastructure gap that exists in Ireland the output elasticity with respect to infrastructure are likely to be higher than those found in other industrialised countries, probably lying in the range between 0.4 to 0.6.
8. The First-time buyers grant, Ir£3 000 (€ 3 809), was abolished. This loss was partially offset by an increase in mortgage interest tax relief for first-time buyers and the extension of the period for which the relief is available from 5 to 7 years.
9. The original act in 2000 limited the life of planning permissions for development purposes to 2 years. This has now been removed and restored to a five year period which will ensure that some planning permissions due to expire have been extended, reducing the imbalance between supply and demand. Furthermore, changes to Part V of the Planning and Development Act will introduce more flexibility into the provision of social and affordable housing, which should encourage the commencement of schemes by developers.
10. See Duffy *et al.* (2001).
11. This would correspond roughly to net immigration of 15 000-20 000 per annum over the coming seven years.
12. However, the nature and scale of the economy means that it would be prudent to maintain a significant safety margin to ensure that an unexpected sharp downturn in economic activity would not push the public finances beyond the deficit limits.
13. For an overview of public expenditure management issues in OECD countries, see Atkinson and Van den Noord (2001).
14. As noted in Chapter II, GNP might better reflects the tax base in Ireland because the presence of highly profitable foreign-owned multinational corporations tends to result in large profit repatriation out of the country (which is counted as GDP but not as GNP). In 2001, the level of GNP amounted to 84 per cent of GDP.
15. International comparisons using gross public social expenditure should be made with care. In most OECD countries including Ireland, public social expenditure is lower on a net (after tax) basis than on a gross (before tax) basis since governments tend to claw back more money through taxation of public transfer income than the value of the tax advantages awarded for social purposes. But the opposite is true for countries such as the United States and Korea. In 1997, net public social expenditure in Ireland was 17.1 per cent of GDP, whereas gross public social expenditure was 19.6 per cent of GDP (Adema, 2001).
16. Of the planned spending, EU transfers will provide about 11 per cent of resources but with a strongly diminishing contribution over the period of programme.
17. Under the terms of the National Pensions Reserve Fund Act, 2001, 1 per cent of GNP is paid annually into the National Pensions Reserve Fund for the pre-funding of the

future cost of social welfare and public service pensions. The Fund's accumulating assets cannot be drawn upon before 2025.

18. The public expenditure guidelines set out in the last Government's Action Programme for the Millennium, published in 1997, were: net current spending growth would be limited to 4 per cent, calculated on an annual average basis; capital spending growth would be limited to 5 per cent on average up to 1999; and overall government spending would be reduced as a share of national output. The present Government elected in June 2002 has not committed to any explicit targets in the Agreed Programme for Government, but has stated that it will respect the commitment under the EU Stability and Growth Pact.

19. According to Honohan (1999) and Power (2002), the reasons for the revenue and expenditure overshooting included conservative budgeting and a propensity to spend any windfall tax receipts in the year in which they arise.

20. National Economic Social Council (2002).

21. It is incremental in the sense that budget was essentially the previous year plus a percentage increase, plus some additional funding for new initiatives.

22. These are projections of the costs of providing the existing levels of services and benefits and projections of revenue assuming no changes in the tax system.

23. Line departments/offices were no longer asked to prepare formal projections for 2003-2005. Instead, the Public Expenditure Division of the Department of Finance carried out an "in-house" exercise into the costs to departments of providing their existing levels of services for those years (2004-2005) according to stated technical guidelines in addition to the costs of contractual and legal commitments entered into by the departments. Consultations took place with Departments on these projections.

24. One exception is the funding in the public transport sector. The Minister for Finance made a five-year funding allocation for public transport in May 2001. It provides for real increases in the current subvention (5 per cent per annum) as well as annual increases of 10 per cent for public transport investment. No other sectors have received such long-term funding commitments.

25. For example, during the early stage of reform in the 1990s, Sweden found that expenditure reviews by the agencies produced universally positive assessments about every aspect of agency activities (OECD, 1997b). In Canada, the process of Programme Review introduced in 1994 helped in prioritising spending only when departments were given targets proposed by the Department of Finance and the Treasury Board Secretariat and approved by ministers. Each department and agency was given a target for expenditure reductions, ranging from 5-60 per cent to be implemented over the coming three years starting with the fiscal year 1995-96. Ministers were then asked to develop programme changes to meet the assigned targets. The process of Programme Review, together with major reforms introduced to the system of transfers to the provinces, is considered to have contributed to fiscal consolidation in Canada during the 1990s (Blöndal, 2001).

26. This was aimed at identifying programmes or projects which no longer justify their cost because of changed circumstances, programmes which could be deferred or delivered over a longer time period, and new delivery or user-charging mechanisms which could improve the management and delivery of programmes.

27. PA Consulting Group (2002).

28. In relation to parliamentary committees, Ministers and Ministers of State would address issues relating to the determination of policy, while Secretaries would address issues relating to the production of outputs.
29. Under the Administrative Budget System, which was introduced in 1991, the Minister for Finance commits to providing an agreed level of administrative spending for a three-year period, while the Minister of the line Department agrees to keep expenditure within the specified limits but has flexibility in managing the expenditure.
30. As of 2002, one department had produced accrual accounts to auditable standard. The remaining departments and offices were at various stages of acquiring and implementing new financial management systems.
31. See Murray (2001) and Humphreys and Worth-Butler (1999).
32. According to one survey, 65 per cent of civil servants believe that under-performance is still left unchallenged with only 10 per cent believing that it has been challenged. Many senior managers argued that they did not have the tools to reward excellence, to improve performance where it is deficient, and to tackle non-performance. In relation to the latter, managers cited organisation culture and potential troubles with unions as being the main constraints which limit their scope for action (PA Consulting Group, 2002).
33. The company holds a 10 year commercial contract with the Department of Transport and is remunerated by way of test and re-test fees.
34. A private company, contracted to manage the new parking restrictions in the Dublin area, is paid an annual fee which is calculated on the basis of the number of hours worked and the number of vehicles on the roads. The proceeds from fines/fees imposed by the company in relation to illegal parking are retained by the Council.
35. These are levied for those patients who do not have a means-tested medical card that provides for free medical care.
36. There are water charges for business/commercial use but not for domestic use. Water charges for domestic use were abolished nationally in 1996.
37. A recent report found that 71 per cent of those in fee-paying secondary schools got into college, compared to 50 per cent in community schools and 38 per cent in vocational schools (Clancy, 2001). It was also found that school-leavers in some middle-class areas were 10 times more likely to go to college than poorer areas.
38. Furthermore, approximately 40 per cent of full-time university students receive maintenance grants. Under the existing system, a student qualifies for a grant if the family income is less than € 21 629. Criticisms have been raised that the means test is defective in that it fails to take full account of ability to pay, particularly since it ignores the accumulated wealth of individuals.
39. 37 per cent of university students were exempt from the charge in 2002. Under current arrangements, few undergraduate students pay tuition fees, so the registration charge is the main third-level cost.
40. A number of Nordic countries operate government-backed student loans, and have one of the highest participation rates in third-level in Europe. The Australian Higher Education Contribution Scheme (HECS), which was first introduced in 1989, has also been considered a very successful case, accompanied by a substantial widening of access. Between 1987 and 1997 total enrolment in Australian universities increased by almost 50 per cent from 441 076 to 658 827; and the percentage of people in the 20-24 age cohort enrolled in a higher education programme increased from 30 per cent

in 1987 to 50 per cent in 1997 (Vossensteyn and Canton, 2001). The primary objective of HECS was to allow the higher education sector to expand without a substantial growth in government funding. In particular, the HECS system was aimed at reintroducing private contributions without jeopardising accessibility to higher education for people from disadvantaged backgrounds. Under the system, students have to contribute approximately a quarter of the average costs of the training programme, either by paying up-front or by taking out a loan and defer repayment through the tax mechanism until after graduation. The experience of these countries suggests that successful implementation is conditional on robust, enforceable repayment arrangements.

41. In Ireland, these local authorities approximate to the general definition of "sub-national government" as used in other OECD countries. However, in Ireland the term "local government" often refers to a broader sub-national administration including such bodies as regional health boards and vocational education committees, which operate outside local authorities. For more details, see OECD (1997a).

42. Department of Environment (1996).

43. Other responsibilities include: management of grants to third-level students, recreation and amenities, and other miscellaneous services.

44. These local or regionally-based bodies operate separately from the local government system and usually have sector-specific executive roles. The main regional bodies include: Health Boards; Vocational Education Committees; County/City Enterprise Boards, and County/City Development Boards.

45. Furthermore, the absence of a local property tax on households has been seen as contributing to inefficient land use by reducing opportunity costs for landowners (OECD, 1999a).

46. In the past, local authorities had to adopt their Estimates without knowing what their funding for general purposes or for non-national roads would be for the following year. Local Government Fund provides guarantees on a legislative basis and Exchequer contributions to local government revenues that are to be increased at least in line with inflation and to take account of any changes in the powers, functions and duties of local authorities.

47. A series of functional, rather than structural, local government reforms have been launched since the early 1990s, which have aimed at creating a modern and efficient local government system. In particular, a document "Better Local Government – A Programme for Change", published in December 1996, put forward a programme for further action on local government reform, which is currently underway.

48. The Local Government Act 1997 established on a statutory basis the Value for Money (VFM) Unit in the Department of the Environment and Local Government, which has carried out VFM studies on local authority operations with a view to boosting efficiency and cost effectiveness. The Value for Money Unit has published twenty-one national studies to date and has circulated them to local authorities who have been asked to implement the recommendations contained therein.

49. These public bodies generally have specific executive or service functions within a particular sector. For example, a significant number of regional bodies operate in the health, tourism promotion and fisheries areas, and more than 100 other local government bodies function at the local level, many supported by EU programmes, and are concerned with rural development, micro enterprises and community development.

50. For example, in the area of employment support policy, the number of actors involved – *i.e.* FAS (national training and employment office), Department of Social and Family

Affairs, local partnerships programmes, social welfare offices, etc. – has often been a problem as the communication channels between the institutions involved and the boundaries between them are not always well defined.

51. For example, Ireland has been developing a catchment based approach in a number of areas for the purpose of investment in wastewater treatment.

52. The present-day system of local government differs little structurally from the one established by the *Local Government* (*Ireland*) *Act*, 1898.

53. Other examples of service improvement include: substantial increases in the number of respite, day and long-stay places available for the physically and intellectually disabled and for the elderly; enhancement of home-based and out-reach mental health units; and development of regional cancer and cardiac services.

54. See Deloitte and Touche (2001).

55. As part of the broadening, the Department of Health and Children would increase the case-mix adjustment rate from 15 per cent to 20 per cent for in-patient cases and from 5 per cent to 7 per cent for day cases. From 2002 these rates would be increased progressively each year.

56. In addition to ten health boards, there is Eastern Regional Health Authority (ERHA). Under the Health (Eastern Regional Health Authority) Act 1999, the Eastern Health Board ceased to exist and the ERHA was established as the statutory body with responsibility to plan, arrange and oversee health and personal social services for the 1.5 million people who leave in three counties – Dublin, Wicklow and Kildare. The services of the ERHA are delivered by three Area Health Boards, the Northern, East Coast and South Western Area Health Boards and by 36 voluntary providers.

57. The establishment of the National Development Plan/Community Support Framework (NDP/CSF) Evaluation Unit, and previously individual Evaluation Units of Government Departments have provided an important structure for systematic, comprehensive evaluations in Ireland.

58. The Government hopes to finance about 5 per cent of the NDP by PPP. In NDP, provision is included for € 2.2 billion of PPP funding including € 1.2 billion for roads and €660 million for environmental projects.

59. PPP programmes are underway in a number of OECD countries including Finland, Germany, Italy, Korea, Mexico, the Netherlands, Portugal, and the United Kingdom.

60. See OECD (2001b).

61. See Figure 3 and Table I.3 in Chapter I of OECD, *Review of Regulatory Reform in Ireland*, 2001.

62. Co-mingling allows cables of different service providers to be mingled in a same building, rather than requiring clear separation of cables by each supplier. Co-mingling thereby reduces costs for competitors to enter local markets.

63. Ireland is also cabled but a main provider lacks the money to enter into competition in the provision of fixed line telephone service.

64. There is of course the north of Ireland and there is an interconnector. But the poor privatisation in the north has resulted in very high generation costs. The cost-benefit analysis on an underwater connection with the UK market is still under way.

65. A VIPP is a company to resell electricity and does not involve any change in ownership or operational control of any generating assets. The instrument allows competitive bidding to the extent that it does not go beyond passing on a certain discount and

there are no incentives to improve generating efficiency. VIPP contract holders can not spill any excess power to the real market, which could form the basis for an admittedly thin market for electricity.

66. To avoid the possibility of ESB frustrating nascent competition from VIPPs through its own VIPP, the ESB is forbidden from any cross subsidisation, exchange of information etc with its subsidiary.

67. As noted in 2001 *Survey*, the Government published in September 2000 a consultation paper which set out a number of reform proposals including the restructuring of CIÉ into a number of separate operating companies. The Government launched a further consultative document in April 2001 which proposed the establishment of a new strategic body for the Greater Dublin Area which would act as public transport regulator. In August 2002, a report by PricewaterhouseCoopers (PwC) provided a review of the financial and other implications of restructuring CIÉ.

68. The White Paper on Adult Education in 1995 set target to raise the figure of 2 per cent of new entrants to higher education over 26 years of age to 15 per cent by the year 2005.

69. This objective is a key indicator in the Community Support Framework 2000-2006 and one of the headline targets of the National Anti-poverty Strategy, the revised document published in February 2002 entitled "Ireland's National Action Plan on Poverty and Social Exclusion" (2002-2007).

70. As of 2000, only 35 per cent of the 55-64 population had completed at least an upper secondary education. This is significantly lower than the OECD average, which is 49 per cent (OECD, Education at Glance 2002).

71. The Skillnets is funded under the National Training Fund, which is financed by a levy on employers of 0.7 per cent of reckonable earning of employees, while the participating companies contribute an average of 32 per cent of the cost of training.

72. According to Callen and Keeney (2002), the replacement rates for a half of employees are 40 per cent or bellow and those for 80 per cent of employees are under 60 per cent. The introduction of minimum wage in 2000 contributed to further reduction in the replacement ratio especially for lower income group by increasing their existing wage levels. A national minimum wage equivalent to Ir pounds 4.4 was introduced in 2000 and was set to rise by the partnership agreement to 4.7 in July 2001 and to 5 in October 2002.

73. Callen and Keeney (2002) show a comparison of the 1998 and 2002 situations in terms of total marginal tax rate. By 2002, about 12 per cent of employees faced a zero marginal tax rate, and about two thirds below 30 per cent. They also estimate the impact of policy changes between 1998 and 2002 on the distribution of total marginal tax rates, measured against some alternative benchmarks. Compared with the scenario under which tax credits and tax bands are assumed to change in line with wage growth so as to keep the average tax rate constant, the actual policy changes enabled over 20 per cent of employees to see their marginal tax rates fall by more than 10 percentage points. Thanks to the widening of the standard rate band and the increased tax-free allowances, more than 160 000 individuals, who would have otherwise faced higher marginal tax rates, have stayed at the same tax bracket and 110 000 individuals have seen their marginal tax rate fall to zero.

74. Since it is only imposed on income above the exemption limit, the marginal relief generates a lower tax bill for low-income workers than the case where standard 20 per cent rate is imposed on all income above the personal allowance. The marginal relief is

phased out at the level of income where the tax bill under the two regimes results in the same amount.

75. Community Employment scheme is targeted at those who remain unemployed for more than 12 months. Vulnerable groups such as people with disabilities, widows and lone parents are also eligible to participate on this scheme subject to the certain criteria with regard to age and unemployment duration.
76. During the period between 1998 and 2002, the number of long-term unemployed (unemployed for 12 months or more) fell from 63.5 thousand to 21.6 thousand, while that of the CE participants declined from 39.5 thousand to 25 thousand.
77. The pilot projects in Kilkenny and Ballyfermot involved referral by the DSCFA of all persons unemployed for more than 6 months to FAS, while the national referral was then limited to only those aged 25 to 34 years who were unemployed for 12 months or more. Between October 1999 and October 2000, Kilkenny experienced 37 per cent drop in unemployment, while that for national level fell only by 20 per cent. See FAS (2002), *The Irish Labour Market Review* 2002.
78. Breakdown of work permit data by nationalities shows that 57 per cent are from non-EEA Europe, 22 per cent from Asia, 8 per cent from Africa and 8 per cent from the North and South America (Ministry of Justice).
79. As of mid 2002, average weekly earnings are € 510 in industry, € 560 in distribution and services, and € 700 in public employment.
80. The average accepted price for electricity from large wind farms was 4.75 eurocents per kilowatt hour. The average price for energy sold by independent producers to the electricity network (the so-called spill price) was 3.47 eurocents in the year to mid 2002.
81. Such a market-determined premium is similar in value to the Danish environmental tax rebate for wind power. The Danish system, however, makes allowance for the costs of maintaining backup power for wind facilities.
82. The pollution caused by these discharges depends on a number of factors such as the timing of the nutrient load, the extent to which the rivers flush the pollution to the sea and growing conditions.

Bibliography

Adema, Willem (2001), "Net Social Expenditure, 2nd Edition", OECD *Labour Market and Social Policy Occasional Papers* No. 52.

Atkinson, P. and P. Van den Noord (2001), "Managing Public Expenditure: Some Emerging Policy Issues and a Framework for Analysis", OECD *Economics Department Working Papers*, No. 285.

Barry, F., and A. Hannon (2001), "Will EU Enlargement Threaten Ireland's Foreign Direct Investment Inflows?", *Quarterly Economic Commentary*, The Economic and Social Research Institute, Winter, pp 55-67.

Bergin, A., J. Fitz Gerald and I. Kearney (2002), "The macro-economic effects of using fiscal instruments to reduce greenhouse gas emissions", *Paper at* ESRI *Energy Policy Research Centre Conference on Efficient and Fair Policies on Global Warming*, 11 December, Dublin.

Blöndal, Jón R. (2001), "Budgeting in Canada", OECD *Journal of Budgeting*, Vol. 1, No.2.

Blondal, S. and S. Scarpetta (1997), "Early retirement in OECD countries: the role of social security systems", OECD *Economic Studies*, No.29.

Blöndal, S., S. Field and N. Girouard (2002), "Investment in Human Capital through Post-Compulsory Education and Training: Selected Efficiency and Equity Aspects", OECD *Economics Department Working Paper* No. 333.

Callan, T., Keeney, M., Walsh, J. (2002), "Budget 2003: Analysis of the Distributional Impact", *Quarterly Economic Commentary*, The Economic and Social Research Institute, Winter, pp. 36-40

Callen, Tim and Mary Keeney (2002), "Taxes, Benefits and the Financial Incentive to Work: Evolution and Policy Impacts", Impact Evaluation of the European Employment Strategy in Ireland.

Cave, Martin (2001), "Voucher Programmes and their Role in Distributing Public Services", OECD *Journal on Budgeting*, Vol. 1, No. 1.

Clancy, Patrick (2001), "College Entry in Focus: A Fourth National Survey of Access to Higher Education", Higher Education Authority.

Commission For Energy Regulation (2002), "Calculation of the 2003 PSO levy", *Information Paper* CER/02/179, 22 October.

Community Support Framework (CSF) Evaluation Unit (1999), *Ex Ante Evaluation of the National Development Plan*, 2000-2006, Dublin.

Comptroller and Auditor General (2001), "Report on Value for Money Examination: The Expenditure Review Initiative", Dublin.

COWI (2002), "Heavy metals in waste", *Report to the European Commission* DG ENV, February, Denmark.

DCFA (Department of Social and family Affairs) 2002, *Actuarial review of the Financial Condition of the Social Insurance Fund*, Government Actuary Department, June 2002. *http://portal.welfare.ie/publications/allpubs/actuarial.pdf*

Deloitte and Touche (2001), "Value for Money Audit of the Irish Health System", June 2001.

Denny, K., and C. Guiomard (1997), "Road Infrastructure and Productivity in Irish Manufacturing", University College Dublin Working Centre for Economic Research Paper No. 97/6.

Department of Environment (1996), *The Financing of Local Government in Ireland*.

Department of the Environment and Local Government (2002), "Making Ireland's development sustainable", *National Report to the World Summit on Sustainable Development*, Dublin, September.

Department of the Taoiseach (2003), *Sustaining Progress: Social Partnership Agreement* 2003-2005, Dublin, February 2003.

Dorgan, S. (2002), Is FDI *necessary in post Celtic Tiger* Ireland?, Strategy Statement, *www.ida.ie/news/showRelease.asp?storyid-28*

Duffy D., J. Fitz Gerald, J. Hore, I. Kearney and C. MacCoille (2001), *Medium-Term Review*, 2001-2007, The Economic and Social Research Institute.

Duffy, D. (2002), A *Descriptive Analysis of the Irish Housing Market*, Quarterly Economic Commentary, The Economic and Social Research Institute, Summer, pp. 40-55.

Environmental Protection Agency (2002a), *Environment in Focus* 2002, February, Wexford.

Environmental Protection Agency (2002b), *Water Quality in Ireland* 1998-2000 , Wexford.

Environmental Resources Management (1998), "Limitations and reduction of CO_2 and other greenhouse gas emissions in Ireland", in association with Byrne O'Cleirigh and Economic and Social Research Institute, Dublin.

EPC-European Policy Committee, (2001), *Budgetary Policy Challenges Posed by an Aging Population*, Brussels, 24thOctober 2001.

Eunomia (2002), "Costs for municipal waste management in the EU", *Final Report to the Directorate General Environment of the European Commission*, Brussels.

European Commission (2002), "Implementation of Council Directive 91/676/EEC concerning the protection of waters against pollution caused by nitrates from agricultural sources", Brussels, July.

FAS (2002), The Irish Labour Market Review 2002.

Honohan, P. (1999), "Fiscal Adjustment and Disinflation in Ireland: Setting the Macro Basis of Economic Recovery and Expansion", in F. Barry (ed.), *Understanding Ireland's Economic Growth*, MacMillan Press.

Honohan, P., B. Maître and C. Conroy (1998), "Invisible Entrepôt Activity in Irish Manufacturing", *Irish Banking Review*, Summer, 22-37.

Hughes, G., P.J O'Connell and J. Williams (2003), "Market Forces and Company Training in Ireland", ESRI Seminar Paper, January.

Humphreys, P. and M. Worth-Butler (1999), "Key Human Resource Management Issues in the Irish Public Service", Committee for Public Management Research Discussion Paper 10.

IEA (2002), *Beyond Kyoto: Energy Dynamics and Climate Stabilisation*, Paris.

LTIG- Long-Term Issues Group (1999), *Long Term Issues Group Paper*, Dublin, Department of Finance

Lundsgaard, J. (2002), "Competition and Efficiency in Publicly Funded Services", OECD *Economics Department Working Paper* No. 331, Paris.

Murray, J. A.(2001), "Reflections on the SMI", The Policy Institute at Trinity College Working Paper, *www.policyinstitute.tcd.ie/publications.html*

National Economic Social Council (2002), "Achieving Quality Outcomes: The Management of Public Expenditure," December 2002.

NDP/CSF Evaluation unit, Department of Finance, (2002), "Employment and Human Resources Development Operational Programme: Evaluation of Provision and Targeting of Measures", July.

Nordhaus W. D. (2001), "Alternative Methods for Measuring Productivity Growth", NBER *Working Paper* No. 8095, January.

O' Leary, J. (2002), "Benchmarking the Benchmarkers", *Quarterly Economic Commentary*, The Economic and Social Research Institute, Winter, pp 77-91.

O'Connell, P.J. (2002), "Are They Working? Market Orientation and the Effectiveness of Active Labour-Market Programmes in Ireland", *European Sociological Review*, Vol. 18, No.1, 65-83.

OECD (1997a), "Ireland", in *Managing Across Levels of Government*, Paris.

OECD (1997b), *Modern Budgeting*, Paris.

OECD (1999a), *Economic Survey of Ireland*, Paris.

OECD (1999b), *Employment Outlook*, Paris.

OECD (2000), OECD *Environmental Performance Reviews: Ireland*, Paris.

OECD (2001a), *Economic Survey of Ireland*, Paris.

OECD (2001b), *Economic Survey of the United Kingdom*, Paris.

OECD (2001c), *Regulatory Reform in Ireland*, Paris.

OECD (2001d), OECD Productivity Manual: A *Guide to the Measurement of Industry-level and Aggregate Productivity growth*, March 2001.

OECD (2002). *Education at a Glance*, Paris.

PA Consulting Group (2002), *Evaluation of the Strategic Management Initiative/Delivering Better Government Modernisation Programme*, Dublin.

Peter Bacon and Associates (2002), *Strategic Review and Outlook for Waste Management Capacity and the Impact on the Irish Economy*, July.

Power, Jim (2002), "Fiscal Management in a Changed Environment", *Quarterly Economic Commentary*, The Economic and Social Research Institute, Summer.

Ruane, F. and R. Lyons (2002), "Wage Determination in the Irish Economy", *Quarterly Economic Commentary*, The Economic and Social Research Institute, Winter 2002, pp 59-76.

Scott, S., J. Curtis, J. Eakins, J. Fitzgerald and J. Hore (2001), *Environmental Accounts: Time Series + Eco-taxes*, ESRI, Dublin, February.

Vossensteyn, Hans and Erik Canton (2001), "Tuition fees and accessibility: the Australian HECS", in S. Uitgevers (ed.), *Higher Education Reform: Getting the Incentives Right*, CPS Netherlands Bureau for Economic Policy Analysis, The Hague.

European Commission, (2002), Statement by the European Commission Representation in Ireland, available at *www.euireland.ie/news/agri/FarmFeature/farmfeature18.htm*

Wiley, Miriam M (2001), "Reform and Renewal of the Irish Health Care System: Policy and Practice", *Budget Perspectives*, The Economic and Social Research Institute.

Annex I

Anti-inflation proposals

An anti-inflation initiative has been proposed as part of the new social partnership agreement *Sustaining Progress* (Department of the Taoiseach, 2003). Proposals for anti-inflation measures are to be co-ordinated by a specially convened group that will draw up a detailed action plan and monitor its progress. Included in the agreement are a number of initiatives agreed by employers and unions, the goal of which is to bring inflation down towards the eurozone average. These initiatives include:

a) More aggressive implementation of competition policy, including dealing with sectors where unnecessary barriers to entry exist.

b) Accelerating studies of the professional services initiated in the wake of the OECD review of Ireland's regulatory regime.

c) Excessive prices are to be tackled by investigations into sectors where price increases do not appear to be justified by market conditions.

d) Action will be taken to reduce the substantial rise in insurance costs.

e) Budgetary policy over the life of the agreement will take account of the proposed inflation target. Public spending should avoid stimulating excess demand in the economy.

f) A public information campaign will be undertaken to improve price awareness amongst consumers.

As a small open economy within a large monetary union inflation in Ireland is significantly determined by external factors, including the exchange rate. Over the medium term, however, proposals to increase competition and investigate sectoral price increases should have an important impact through productivity improvement and a check on pricing powers of quasi-monopoly in certain sectors. Furthermore, the consumer price index has in recent years reflected administered price changes that include a rise in excise duty on tobacco and a series of public service price increases. If, however, domestically generated inflation is to be effectively tackled, then measures should also be aimed both at reducing excess demand and increasing the economy's supply capacity.

Annex II

Social partnership in Ireland

The original impetus for the current series of agreements came from the poor state of the economy and the public finances in the mid to late 1980s. In 1987, the newly elected government set about correcting the public finances through relatively stringent cuts in public expenditure. The Programme for National Recovery (PNR), the first of the current type of agreements, was a key part of the process and a central element of the Programme was a desire to achieve consensus on wage bargaining and deliver a cost/wage structure that would enhance the competitiveness of the economy. This model was based on agreement between the social partners – government, employers and trade unions – to limit wage increases in return for other concessions. Initially the centrepiece of the concessions was a gradual reduction in the personal tax burden. This model has persisted ever since, but subsequently the negotiations have widened to include agricultural organisations and community groups and the final agreements have broadened to include social and community issues. Nonetheless, employees of multinational companies have not been a party to this process.

Figure A1 compares the rates of centrally agreed wage increase and actual outturns for the three sectors for which wage data are available on the basis of unchanged employment structure. It shows that the wage terms of the agreements have generally been exceeded by significant margins. However, the centralised bargaining nature of the agreements probably contributed to reducing industrial unrest.

Figure A1. **Social partnership agreements**

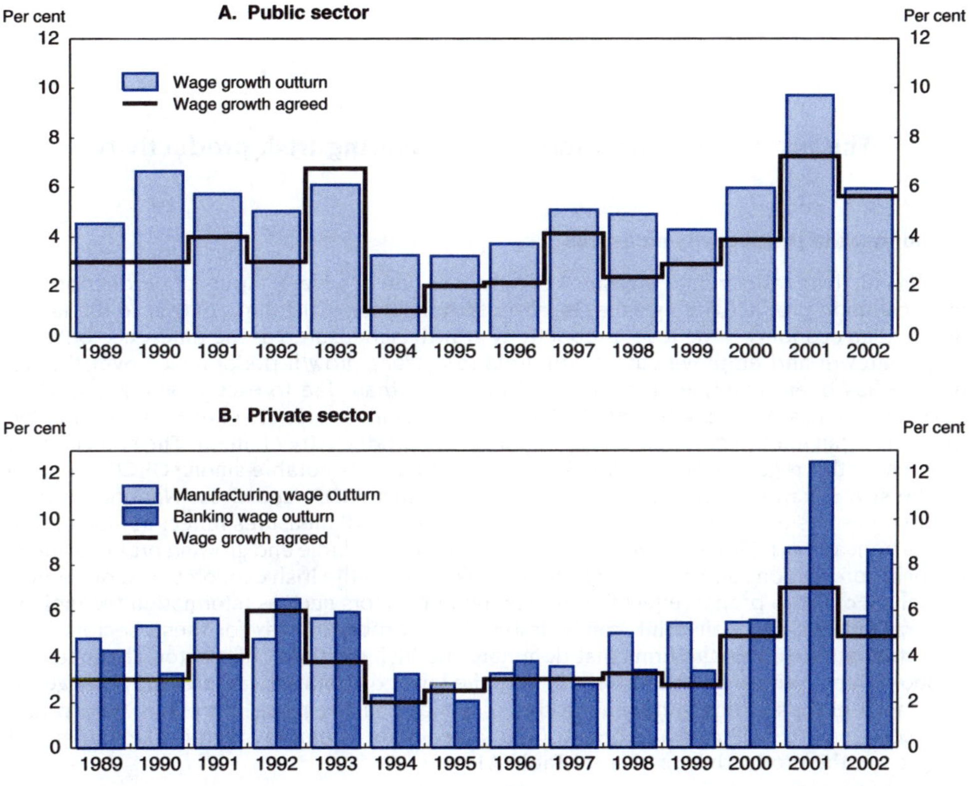

Sources: Ministry of Finance and CSO.

Annex III
The problems associated with measuring Irish productivity

Economy-wide productivity measures

Productivity ratios relate measures of output to one or several inputs of production. The most common productivity measure is labour productivity, which links output to the labour input. At an economy–wide level productivity growth is measured as the difference between output growth and employment growth. Ireland's strong growth performance over the last decade has been mainly employment-driven rather than due to exceptional productivity growth which has been healthy rather than miraculous in nature. There are a number of factors, which can lead to potential exaggeration of the productivity element. The source of the problem in this regard is how output is measured. Ireland is notable among OECD countries for the size of gap between its Gross Domestic Product (GDP) and Gross National Product (GNP) measures of output. The gap between GDP and GNP measures reflect net factor payments from abroad. These payments are dominated by the large and growing profits of multinational corporations and act as a significant leakage from the Irish economy. The problem is that much of these profits reflect the high margin in sectors such as information technology, pharmaceuticals and soft drink concentrates. Low corporation tax for these sectors is an important attraction for the firms that dominate the Irish multinational sector. The incentive to book large profits in Ireland to benefit from the lower corporation tax rates may exaggerate how much of these firms' net value added is actually taking place in Ireland. As a consequence using the GDP measure of output for given level of employment is likely to greatly exaggerate the productivity measure (Table A1).

Table A1. **Productivity growth**
Per cent

	Using output measure	
	Real GDP	Real GNP
1996	4.5	4.2
1997	7.0	5.6
1998	0.5	–0.1
1999	4.8	2.5
2000	5.3	6.0
2001	2.8	1.7

Source: CSO National Accounts and the Quarterly National Household Survey.

Aggregating productivity growth across industries

This same problem of productivity measurement in Ireland is also found when attempting to aggregate productivity growth across industries. The basic procedure is to use a quantity index for industry as a whole where each industry is weighted by its gross value added as a proportion of the total (OECD, 2001d). The problem of measurement is again related to the large share of multi-national presence in the Irish economy. Foreign-owned multinational corporations (MNCs) represent a higher share of manufacturing capacity in Ireland than in any other EU country. In particular, the "three C's" (computing, chemicals and cola-concentrates) dominate manufacturing output growth. The chemical sector currently has a weighting of over 30 per cent in volume terms measured by gross value added. In volume terms, industrial production for manufacturing industries has increased by about 180 per cent between 1995 and 2002. However, if the chemicals sector is excluded for instance, growth is reduced significantly to less than 80 per cent over that period.

Multinationals dominate the chemicals sector and a huge proportion of the value added is attributable to the profits of those companies. Many of these companies are characterised by a relatively low labour share and only a small proportion of the gross value added is distributed to the domestic workforce. Therefore their high levels of output are not reflected in Irish incomes. However, when analysing production growth, we cannot exclude a sector that appears to account for such a large proportion of total industry. A more appropriate way to deal with this bias in the production figures is not to exclude the sectors that are contributing to the bias but to use wage bill weights rather than output weights for each industry, thereby taking into consideration the real effect on the economy from the various productivity gains. Using wage bill weights as opposed to output weights for the various industries, production increased by about 115 per cent over the period 1995 to 2002 (Table A2). This again is a significant reduction compared to the 180 per cent increase when using only output weights.

Sectors with high multi-national presence, like the chemical and ICT sectors, are also characterised by the high return on capital and the high use of non-industrial services, which include royalties and consultancy fees. This implies that, in addition to physical materials and the other standard forms of inputs, this segment of Irish manufacturing is using invisible or immaterial resources to generate the measured value of output. These immaterial

Table A2. **Volume indices of production: manufacturing**

Index 1995 = 100

	Output weighted	Wage-bill weighted	% change from Nov. 1994[1]	
			Output weighted	Wage bill weighted
1994-Nov.	91.09	94.22	0	0
1995-Nov.	111.10	109.90	22	17
1996-Nov.	123.43	120.81	36	28
1997-Nov.	146.58	136.30	61	45
1998-Nov.	169.80	153.23	86	63
1999-Nov.	198.13	167.91	118	78
2000-Nov.	241.06	199.56	165	112
2001-Nov.	220.80	183.01	142	94
2002-Nov.	252.22	203.27	177	116

1. This period is used in order to make annual comparisons with the most recently available data, *i. e.* November 2002

Source: ESRI.

resources reflect technological, scientific/market knowledge, brands and other elements, which contribute to market power and market value. These have been called "invisible entrepôts" due to the way these intangible factors arrive and leave like cargoes. These intangibles are not substantially modified in the process but are required for the activities of some of the manufacturing sectors and can generate significant value added to production. The owners of these immaterial factors, usually a parent or associate of the entity that is manufacturing in Ireland, are rewarded by royalties, license fees and dividends and other distributions. These immaterial factors are present in all economies but Irish manufacturing relies on them to a greater extent than others because of the extent of foreign ownership and the modest extent to which these sources of market value are actually generated in Ireland through processes like research and development (R&D). The consequence of a high degree of non-industrial services in the sectoral net output measure is that it exaggerates the value added taking place in Ireland resulting in inflated productivity measures.

The sectors that dominate the industrial sector in Ireland tend to be characterised by low labour shares and high purchase of non-industrial services. In 2001, the industrial (including buildings) sector accounted for over 40 per cent of gross value added, the base for GDP measures. Within the industrial sector, three sub-sectors with exceptionally low labour shares of production values in the latest Census of Industrial Production for 1999 were cola concentrates (NACE 1589), reproduction of computer media (NACE 2233) and organic basic chemicals (NACE 2414). These three sub-sectors accounted for over one-third of gross value added in the industrial sector in 1999. They have very high productivity in terms of production values to numbers employed, while the ratio of labour cost to non-industrial services is very high in contrast to other sector in the manufacturing industries (Table A3).

In general, the pitfalls to output measurement and therefore productivity growth are numerous and complex for a small open economy with such large multinational presence. In international comparisons Ireland has seen exceptional productivity growth when measured by labour productivity but this has been largely due to the large multinational presence (maximised by the use of GDP in productivity calculations). This is compounded by the unusual structure of its manufacturing sector, in particular the dominance of the chemical sector. The supposed productivity gains are often not translated in comparable gains for Irish incomes and are therefore largely overstated. More appropriate productivity measures should not exclude the sectors causing the exaggerated productivity growth in making calculations but instead turn to new productivity measures which account for multiple factor inputs (Nordhauss, 2001). Also, much productivity growth differences across industries are due to differences in unmeasured inputs and therefore a more suitable measure would be a chain index of productivity growth of the different sectors weighted by expenditure or current-value input shares.

Table A3. **Productivity and entrepôt type activities**

	Productivity	Entrepôt Indicator
	Production value per employee	Labour cost/Non-industrial services costs
	Ir£'000s	%
Cola-concentrate	1 803.4	2.9
Organic chemicals	2 072.4	5.3
Reproduction of computer media	981.8	5.8
Other manufacturing	178.7	97.6

Source: CSO Census of Industrial Production 1999.

BASIC STATISTICS

BASIC STATISTICS:

INTERNATIONAL COMPARISONS

	Units	Reference period[1]	Australia	Austria	Belgiu
Population					
Total	Thousands	2000	19 157	8 110	10226
Inhabitants per sq. km	Number	2000	2	97	335
Net average annual increase over previous 10 years	%	2000	1.2	0.5	0.3
Employment					
Total civilian employment (TCE)[2]	Thousands	2000	9 048	3730 (99)	3858
of which:					
Agriculture	% of TCE	2000	4.9	6.2 (99)	2.2
Industry	% of TCE	2000	22.0	30.6 (99)	24.7
Services	% of TCE	2000	73.1	63.2 (99)	68.2
Gross domestic product (GDP)					
At current prices and current exchange rates	Bill. USD	2000	388.5	188.7	228.8
Per capita	USD	2000	20 158	23 270	22 330
At current prices using current PPPs[3]	Bill. USD	2000	507.6	219.0	268.3
Per capita	USD	2000	26 338	27 001	26 190
Average annual volume growth over previous 5 years	%	2000	3.9	2.6	2.8
Gross fixed capital formation (GFCF)	% of GDP	2000	22.7	23.6	20.7
of which:					
Machinery and equipment	% of GDP	2000	...	8.0	9.2
Residential construction	% of GDP	2000	4.5	5.4	4.5
Average annual volume growth over previous 5 years	%	2000	0.5	0.2	0.8
Gross saving ratio[4]	% of GDP	2000	18.3	21.8	26.2
General government					
Current expenditure on goods and services	% of GDP	2000	18.2	19.0	20.5
Current disbursements[5]	% of GDP	2000	32.1 (98)	46.9	46.8
Current receipts[6]	% of GDP	2000	33.7 (98)	47.1	47.8
Net official development assistance	% of GNI	2000	0.27	0.23	0.36
Indicators of living standards					
Private consumption per capita using current PPPs[3]	USD	2000	15 829	14 910	13 831
Passenger cars, per 1000 inhabitants	Number	1999	510 (98)	496	448
Internet subscribers, per 100 inhabitants	Number	2000	12.7	6.00	10.6
Television sets, per 1000 inhabitants	Number	1998	548 (97)	331	340
Doctors, per 1000 inhabitants	Number	1999	2.5 (98)	3.0	3.8
Infant mortality per 1000 live births	Number	1999	5.7	4.4	5.3
Wages and prices (average annual increase rate over previous 5 years)					
Wages (earnings or rates according to availability)	%	2001	2.8	2.5	2.5
Consumer prices	%	2001	2.3	1.6	1.7
International trade[7]					
Exports of goods, fob	Mill. USD	2000	63 920	64 226	187 957
As % of GDP	%	2000	16.5	34.0	82.1
Average annual increase rate over previous 5 years	%	2000	3.8	2.2	1.4
Imports of goods, cif	Mill. USD	2000	67 742	69 058	177 121
As % of GDP	%	2000	17.4	36.6	77.4
Average annual increase rate over previous 5 years	%	2000	3.4	0.8	2.1
Total official reserves[8]	Mill. SDR's	2000	15 455	11 017	7 969
As ratio of average monthly imports of goods	Ratio	2000	2.7	2.1	0.5

1. Unless otherwise stated.
2. According to the definitions used in OECD *Labour Force Statistics*.
3. PPPs = Purchasing Power Parities.
4. Gross Saving = Gross national disposable income minus private and government consumption.
5. Current disbursements = General government final consumption expenditure plus subsidies plus property income plus current taxes on income, wealth, etc. plus social benefits other than transfers in kind plus other current transfers.
6. Current receipts = Operating surplus plus taxes on production and imports plus property income plus current taxes on income, wealth, etc. plus social contributions plus other current transfers.

OECD PUBLICATIONS, 2, rue André-Pascal, 75775 PARIS CEDEX 16
PRINTED IN FRANCE
(10 2003 09 1 P) ISBN 92-64-10297-3 – No. 53121 2003
ISSN 0376-6438